# PLACEMAKERS

# MAKERS

EMPERORS     KINGS     ENTREPRENEURS

*A Brief History of
Real Estate Development*

HERB AUERBACH
*with* IRA NADEL

**Figure 1**
*Vancouver / Berkeley*

*Dedicated to my wife*
MARY ALLISON JAMES AUERBACH

**Previous page:** *This Must Be the Place*, by Roy Lichtenstein, might well have been inspired by the placemakers of today and the artist's vision of what real estate development would look like in the future.

Cataloguing data available from Library and Archives Canada
ISBN 978-1-927958-79-7 (hbk.)

Copy editing by Judy Phillips
Proofreading by Eva van Emden
Indexing by Stephen Ullstrom
Author photographs by Paul H. Auerbach (top) and Edward Chang (bottom)
Photo research by John Calimente
Front jacket photograph courtesy of Place Ville Marie
Back jacket photographs: see page 197 for permissions
Printed and bound in China by C&C Offset Printing Co., Ltd.
Distributed in the U.S. by Publishers Group West

*Placemakers* was published with the generous support of Simon Fraser University

Figure 1 Publishing Inc.
Vancouver BC Canada
www.figure1pub.com

**CONTENTS**

## *Preface*

THIS BOOK IS a personal look at history through the lens of real estate development, populated by stories from biblical times to the present and beyond. Geographically, *Placemakers* spans the globe, from the Middle East to Europe and North America, making side trips to China and even outer space. Each chapter focuses on a different era; the narrative emphasizes selected real estate projects and the "placemakers" who made them and shows the influence social trends had on these projects, as well as the reverse.

For example, the development of the railroad in the nineteenth century enabled the movement of goods and people. At the same time, it encouraged land development near, over or abutting rail lines and stations. However, in North America, rail transportation of people was soon superseded by the automobile, which made possible the real estate development of suburbia and the shopping mall.

My interest in real estate development derives from my lengthy career as an architect working with developers and later as a real estate development manager and consultant. My interest in the history of real estate development and placemakers began when I included the subject in my course Real Estate Development from the Inside Out, which I have been teaching at Simon Fraser University in Vancouver since 1991. Of course, I may not be objective, but I find most folks seem to be interested in real estate and real estate development. How else can you account for the large percentage of time (and space) this subject takes up in the media, or the billion people worldwide who have played Monopoly (the board game is reported to be published in forty-seven languages and sold in 114 countries)? I personally find history fascinating, and hope the description of certain historical events through their links to real estate will interest readers and prompt them to explore the topic further.

Over centuries, real estate developers have received a bad rap. Granted, plenty of examples of poor real estate developments justify such criticism. But few people realize the creativity and risk inherent in development, and the bad rap is not always warranted. Accordingly, where appropriate, this book censures some real estate developers, but for the most part celebrates these "placemakers" and their herculean accomplishments.

*Placemakers* is not a complete history of real estate development. Rather, it is a collection of stories from historical periods related to real estate projects and developers, supplemented by stories from my own experience. The examples showcased are those that have intrigued me during my architectural or consulting career and in some cases directly involved me. I have also drawn from a range of books and essays that have informed my understanding of real estate development from its beginnings. The Selected Bibliography at the end of the book lists them.

The chief focus, however, is the people—the placemakers who made development happen, from Emperor Augustus of ancient Rome, who shaped the world's largest city into an imperial capital; to Louis XIII's Cardinal Richelieu, who introduced the seigneurial system along the St. Lawrence River in Quebec and developed his own town in southern France; to Napoleon III, ruler of the Second French Empire, who through his planner Baron Haussmann put his indelible stamp on the city of Paris. The characters profiled stem from different backgrounds but were all, in their way, "placemakers" who had an impact on history and on our physical world today.

*Herb Auerbach*
VANCOUVER, B.C.
FEBRUARY 1, 2016

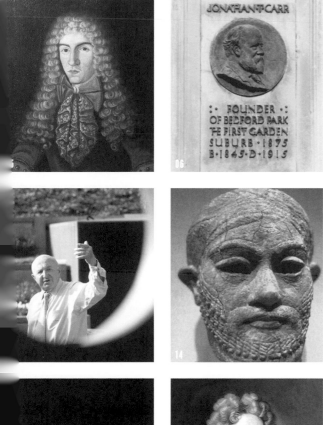

JONATHAN·T·CARR

·:· FOUNDER ·:·
OF BEDFORD PARK
TE FIRST GARDEN
SUBURB ·1875·
B·1845·D·1915

06

07

08

14

15

16

22

23

24

| | | | | | |
|---|---|---|---|---|---|
| **01** | Alexander the Great | **09** | Job Harriman | **17** | Richard Norman Shaw |
| **02** | Emperor Augustus | **10** | Baron Haussmann | **18** | Al Smith |
| **03** | Alice Constance Austin | **11** | Henry VIII | **19** | Van Sweringen Brothers |
| **04** | Tommaso Campanella | **12** | Bill Levitt | **20** | Emperor Taizu |
| **05** | Prince Carafa | **13** | Raymond Nasher | **21** | Donald Trump |
| **06** | Jonathan Carr | **14** | King Ur-Nammu | **22** | Christopher Wren |
| **07** | King Camp Gillette | **15** | Napoleon III | **23** | Frank Lloyd Wright |
| **08** | Victor Gruen | **16** | Cardinal Richelieu | **24** | William Zeckendorf |

# Introduction

*Avon Owns TIffany*

*"Avon owns Tiffany?" she gasped. "I can't handle this!"*
*And with that, one of the students, whom I judged to be about thirty years old, fled my classroom. Her abrupt exit occurred while I was in the midst of discussing the importance of land in the real estate development course I teach at Vancouver's Simon Fraser University. I was explaining how Donald Trump had acquired the land and air rights he needed to build the glitzy Manhattan apartment building that bears his name: Trump Tower. After all, ownership rights are the key to real estate development.*

THE ICONIC New York jewelry store Tiffany & Co. sits triumph-
antly on Fifth Avenue between Fifty-sixth and Fifty-seventh
Streets in a low building that has unused air rights. Because
Tiffany never intended to rebuild on the site, its valuable air
rights, which could only be transferred to an abutting property,
might have otherwise remained idle—an unrealized asset.

Donald Trump bought air rights
from Tiffany & Co. in the 1970s
so he could add more floors to
his Trump Tower next door.

However, in the late 1970s, in order to take advantage of
this unrealized asset, Donald Trump, real estate wheeler and
dealer par excellence, made a deal with the then owner of the
Tiffany store to acquire the unbuilt air rights, so he, Trump,
could add floors to his new building on his own site next door.
More floors were desirable because the value of each floor went
up the higher they rose and the better the view. But when it
came time for Tiffany to sign a formal agreement so Trump
could secure a building permit, he learned that Tiffany had
been sold to Avon Cosmetics, and Avon would not honor what
had been a handshake deal between Trump and Tiffany's previous owner.

When Avon, the queen of door-to-door cosmetics, bought
Tiffany in 1979 for over $100 million, Wall Street wondered if the
marriage would last. It did not, and in 1984, Avon sold Tiffany.

As it turned out, back in 1979, Tiffany's prior owner, a
refined and honorable English gentleman, did convince Avon
to honor the deal he had made with Trump. As a result, the air
rights were sold and transferred, and Trump built the extra
floors. One has to wonder whether Trump's second daughter, Tiffany, was named in gratitude for, and in honor of,
that deal. However grateful Donald Trump might have been
to Tiffany, he nonetheless went on to name the tower after

himself. Naming a building after oneself—if not a whole town or city, as you will learn in this book—is a fairly common practice of real estate developers who seek identity, recognition and posterity.

What Trump had to go through to secure air rights from Tiffany is just one example of the hurdles real estate developers have to overcome and have had to overcome through the ages. Above all, developers must be able to respond to the realities of the times. In the case of Trump Tower, Trump was a temporary victim of the rash of mergers and acquisitions and leveraged buyouts that took place in the 1970s, including the sale of Tiffany.

It is commonplace in real estate development that just when a developer sees the "finish line," someone or some entity erects another obstacle. Hurdles and obstacles feature in every project; a developer cannot predict them all and rarely knows when one will appear to delay, and in some instances even scuttle, a project. As they pursue their various goals, real estate developers may find themselves battling diverse opponents, including hostile communities, impatient lenders, new civic leaders, natural disasters and changing market conditions.

Had Donald Trump taken my course, he would have learned about William Lever, Britain's leading soap manufacturer and developer of the utopian company town of Port Sunlight, England. In 1917, he attempted to purchase the Isle of Lewis, off the coast of Scotland, in order to build another utopian town, this one centered not on soap but on a fishing cannery. Lewis Islanders would have none of it, and Lever was forced to abandon his plans. Little did he know that among the opponents might have been some of Donald Trump's relatives.

As of this writing, in honor of his mother, who was born on the Isle of Lewis, Trump is trying to develop those same lands in

Scotland as the world's largest and most luxurious golf course complex. He too has been running into difficulties with a hostile community and holdout property owners, who refuse to be intimidated by power and wealth.

Despite such obstacles, developers are often tenacious—and patient. And they share other character traits that this book aims to highlight in trying to understand what drives them on. From ancient times, across the centuries, there have always been visionaries: builders, planners and developers who I like to call "placemakers." Their motives vary, ranging from imperial might to religious fervor to commercial greed. The developers of "picturesque villages" and company towns in the 1800s had the welfare of everyday commuters and employees at heart. From kings to zealots to entrepreneurs, together developers present an interesting bunch, indeed, characters on a mission and who often seem larger than life.

## A BUSINESS LEARNED BY DOING

Unlike architecture, engineering and other recognized professions, real estate development at first had no schools to provide training or grant degrees. It has been, and remains, a business learned by doing. Several universities now offer courses in real estate development as a profession. However, many of these courses focus only on asset management and fail to teach the creative elements of real estate development, leaving unanswered questions such as "Where does the vision come from?" or "How do you add value to land?" And "adding value" is what real estate developers try to do by determining highest- and best-use scenarios and then, more often than not, having to secure the entitlements necessary to realize these possibilities.

# 01

# Why We Build

*The instinct to build can be traced to the Neolithic age, some eight thousand years ago, when adult men piled large stones one upon another to make shelters or mark sacred places. Meanwhile, young boys piled small stones upon small stones simply to play at building. The first man-made blocks were found in the Walls of Jericho (ca. 8000 BCE), and children have continued to play with blocks ever since. Although I cannot remember that far back in my own youth, I know my children and grandchildren all started building at a very early age. They loved stacking blocks into towers, built castles in the sand, and then graduated from Lincoln Logs to Erector sets to Lego.*

*During the Middle Ages, boys hanging about woodworking shops no doubt picked up small pieces of wood to use as building blocks. The first known manufactured wooden building blocks date to the 1600s. Six hundred locations worldwide now feature Rockwell's Imagination Playgrounds, inviting kids to collaborate to build their own structures out of hundreds of large soft blue components.*

*So we all love to build, but not all of us end up being builders.*

LOOK AROUND YOU. You live in a house or an apartment, you work in an office or a factory, you shop along a main street or in a mall, you spend leisure time in a community center, gym or theater. You may attend a place of worship or a school; you may visit interesting buildings and cities when you travel. We all live, work and relax in built environments, yet few of us who are not in the business, unless we have built our own home or cabin, appreciate what goes into the acquisition of land and the building of buildings. Nor do we know who built these structures or know the history of real estate development, the world's second-oldest profession. I refer to those adventurous individuals as "placemakers," those real estate developers who, along with architects and investors, took risks to fashion skyscrapers, residential lots, whole cities or shopping malls. They created palaces, fortresses and homes. They gave space an identity.

Humans have been building for thousands of years, but not until some six thousand years ago did they stop roaming about, stay in one place and start to build cities. Apart from providing a place to live, those early cities were built for one of three reasons: to provide protection, to facilitate trade or to celebrate a sacred place, either religious or royal. The building of cities was, in fact, an act of real estate development and placemaking by royal, clerical or government developers who built for purposes other than to make money. Although speculative developers built apartments in ancient Rome (see chapter 5), often with disastrous consequences, not until the Renaissance did real estate development for a profit emerge as a major business. Whether for profit or not, real estate development, in both ancient times and today, has always been a creative enterprise whose object is to "add value" to properties by either building on them or renovating and upgrading existing buildings.

There are many species other than "man" that build, and many of them build elaborate and complex structures. Yet only those structures built by "man" have had a negative effect on the environment—if you exclude the beaver's lodge, which requires the cutting of trees and damming of rivers. Like his fellow creatures, "man" builds for similar reasons: for shelter, just as an eagle builds an aerie; or for protection, just as an amoeba creates a shell; or for industrial purposes, the same reason bees construct a hive.

Where does the human building instinct come from? It is one thing to build for shelter, protection, trade or religion, but quite another to build for profit, recognition and glory. However, with the exception of man, the way other species have built has remained the same for eons. By contrast, since man built the first hut, he has had the insatiable desire to build bigger and higher, from the pyramids in Egypt and the Pharos in Alexandria (see page 52), the tallest structures of the ancient world, to Burj Khalifa, Dubai, the world's tallest building today. In China, there is currently a plan to construct a building a mile (1.6 km) high. No creature other than man has tried to improve their building methods or build "bigger" or build to celebrate a sacred place, with two notable exceptions: the termite and the bowerbird (see sidebars).

Man as builder is motivated not only by primordial instincts to protect and shelter himself, but also by his ego, sometimes greed and occasionally altruism. Since the beginning of time, man has been on a path of forever trying to improve the cave, and as early as the construction of the Ziggurat of Ur in 3000 BCE (see page 41), man built for posterity and celebrity. Building for posterity is a way to live on after death, and most placemakers strive for a positive legacy. After all, it is often said that although doctors can bury their mistakes, architects, builders and real estate developers cannot.

When a company puts its name on a building, such as the Chrysler Building in New York City, it does so for identification and advertising purposes. But when developers put their name on a building or project, such as Trump Tower or Levittown (see chapter 15), they are driven by ego and a search for recognition and posterity. Sponsors who finance such structures also seek recognition. Alexander the Great (see chapter 4) insisted on having all structures in his realm, not to mention the city he built, named after him. It would please him to learn that there are now some thirty cities in the world named Alexandria. In modern times, naming buildings has become an epidemic: apartment houses, concert halls, business towers, shopping centers, libraries and even bridges are named after individuals.

We have seen some of the reasons behind humans' driving force to build. But over time, what are the conditions that produce the modern-day real estate developer or placemaker? What does it take to be a placemaker? Throughout history, those who developed real estate possessed a number of distinct characteristics and advantages.

**CREATIVITY —**
The ability to envision the future and see the potential of "what could be" as opposed to "what was" and "what is."

**ACCESS TO POWER AND WEALTH —**
To drive and fund that vision.

**OPTIMISM —**
A belief that their projects could be achieved.

**THE TENDENCY TO DREAM —**
In many cases, developers were utopians and dreamers who did not want to be awakened.

**EXTREME SELF-CONFIDENCE —**
They were often the sole or eldest son, encouraged to be achievers by ambitious parents.

**EXCELLENT PEOPLE AND MANAGEMENT SKILLS —**
Able to organize human, material and financial resources.

**GREAT SALES SKILLS —**
Able to convince financers, purchasers, lessors, communities and authorities of the viability and desirability of their projects.

**THE ABILITY TO "THINK BIG" —**
Capable of dealing with the array of challenges confronting every project, including technical, aesthetic, legal, marketing and, of course, financial problems.

**A BELIEF THAT THEIR PROJECTS HAD MERIT —**
Whether they were George Cadbury building a company town, Donald Trump constructing a tower or William Levitt shaping a suburb, these developers all believed their projects aided the public good.

In reference to that final trait, we all understand that the developer's view of serving the public good does not always match the public's view, nor that of the local authorities.

Many projects have been disasters, the most noted of which was the Pruitt-Igoe social housing project in St. Louis, Missouri. The "urban renewal" movement in the United States after World War II—under which federal funds became available to remake vast slum areas, many of them black neighborhoods—meant the demolition of large areas in order to build massive housing projects. Pruitt-Igoe was one, developed in 1950 by the St. Louis Housing Authority.

Designed by Minoru Yamasaki, architect of the World Trade Center towers, the thirty-three Pruitt-Igoe apartment towers, set to be a model of modern social housing, opened in 1954. However, housing alone does not solve social problems. First, the project was segregated, one portion named after one of the first African-American pilots of the famed Tuskegee Airmen, Wendell O. Pruitt, and the other portion, for white residents, after Missouri congressman William L. Igoe. There were never sufficient funds for maintenance and security, and the projects began to suffer from deterioration, vandalism and crime. By the mid-1960s, the buildings became unlivable, and a decade later all of them were demolished, the entire project a sad example of the failure of urban renewal, development and public policy.

Today, because of such past failures, many projects come under greater public scrutiny and have to submit to extensive public hearings and consultations before construction. They are subject to planning department reviews and design review panels. Developers must provide detailed studies and statements concerning the impact of the project on the environment, the neighborhood and the economy. I believe these new constraints have forced developers to become more "professional" and have resulted for the most part in better buildings and better placemaking. Although the delays lengthen the process, they also result in better designed buildings largely accepted by the public.

Despite such obstacles, real estate developers continue
to launch project after project, feeding a seemingly insatiable
appetite to find new opportunities, which has increased the
need for more land on which they can build. In the past and in
the present, it is rare for a person with the developer instinct to
pass a vacant piece of land or an underutilized building without
asking, "What can I build on that property?" or "How could I
better utilize that building?" As the following chapters reveal,
developers and placemakers have brought their vision to life.

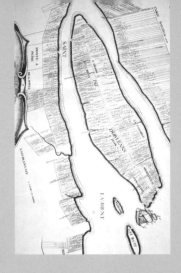

# 02 Land and Laws

*In order to build, you need the "right" to build—whether on land, in midair or on a water lot—by having either title or a lease. Yet acquiring land is not always easy and can be fraught with obstacles. What follows is a personal story about one such obstacle.*

*I had lunch one day with the holdout owner of a corner property that my development company was trying to acquire as part of a larger land assembly. I explained that if we developed the parcels we already had options on, not much could be built on his parcel and it would be worth less. By having assembled the other parcels, we could build a major building on the land, and by adding the corner property, enhance the value of the project. Accordingly, I was able to offer him a good price for his land. He accepted, and I said, "That's a deal. I need an option." He said, "You've got it!" and shook my hand, which is how real estate deals are often done.*

*Shortly after, we received the requisite option document from his lawyer, designed the building, secured a major tenant and received a financing commitment from a pension fund. When it came time to close (complete the transaction) on the corner property, there was a glitch; one of those obstacles appeared. A third party surfaced, claiming they owned the property, and presented evidence that the owner had pledged the parcel to them without registering the pledge against title.*

*In the end, however, much like Trump's handshake deal with Tiffany, the owner honored his commitment by paying off the claimant. We closed on the property and built the building.*

*Securing clear title to land is just one of the many obstacles builders and developers must overcome. In addition to ownership of the land, developers need the right or "entitlement" to build on it. But never make assumptions. And always expect the unexpected.*

THE IDEA OF OWNING PROPERTY came with the end of nomadic life some ten thousand years ago. Settling in one place made possible the production of surplus food, collective living and the development of specialized trades, which led to the establishment of permanent settlements. For two thousand years our ancestors lived in small clusters, more complex compounds and finally in villages. Another three thousand years passed before they started to build cities. But thousands of years later, once people were settled in towns, villages and cities, nomadic genes kicked in once more and, thanks to the art of shipbuilding (and the salting of cod, which preserved the fish and made long sea voyages possible), they started traveling to trade, to explore and to find new opportunities, which for some meant to conquer, claim and possess land.

In the process, humans who were being crowded, were being religiously persecuted or were not permitted to own land discovered new lands, which only increased their appetite for more land. By the 1400s, exploration expanded in the search for new markets. By the 1600s, many more sought religious freedom. By the 1700s and 1800s, the new Industrial Revolution required greater resources as it produced greater wealth; the demand for more goods and resources increased, much of it coming from abroad. Europe was becoming crowded, and migrations occurred to secure land, resources and new opportunities. The availability of new lands and the growing needs of industry and for housing encouraged more real estate development in Europe and beyond.

Real estate development and placemaking requires not only the control of land but also institutions and laws that will ensure title to protect that ownership or control. Although the idea of personal property emerged at the end of nomadic life, the concepts of title and laws to protect it originated in biblical times—as illustrated by the story of Abraham and the establishment of the Tombs of the Patriarchs.

Not until the end of nomadic life did villages, towns and then cities develop, creating the need for real estate.

THE TOMBS OF THE PATRIARCHS in Hebron (now in the West Bank) is a shrine complex built mainly under Herod, the king of Judaea, in the first century BCE, with additions by the Crusaders in the twelfth century CE. It centers on the Cave of Machpelah, an ancient double cave revered since at least 1000 BCE as the burial site of the Hebrew patriarchs Abraham, Isaac and Jacob and their wives. Recent excavations of the double cave revealed artifacts from the early Israelite Period (some thirty centuries ago). The great wall that still surrounds the Cave of Machpelah was built by Herod the Great from 34 to 31 BCE.

How did the Tombs of the Patriarchs come to be? Cemeteries have always been lucrative real estate ventures and probably represented an early form of subdivision, generating big bucks on a dollar-per-square-foot basis. According to the Bible, when Abraham's wife Sarah died at the age of 127, Abraham wanted to bury her in a cave near where they came from, in what was

Abraham, by purchasing a burial site for his wife Sarah at what became the Tombs of the Patriarchs, demonstrated the importance of fee simple ownership.

then called Canaan. At the time, the area was controlled by the sons of Heth, who would not "sell" but would only "lease" the gravesite to Abraham. The prophet knew the value of fee simple ownership and having title and that is why, as Sarah lay dead in the Cave of Machpelah, he negotiated for four years with the sons of Heth, until he was able to purchase the gravesite from them in perpetuity. He paid ten times its value to secure fee simple ownership, and that gravesite and the cave became known as the Tombs of the Patriarchs.

The Bible contains numerous real estate references: Abraham's quest for a gravesite can be found in Genesis; Leviticus talks about title, ownership and foreclosure; Joshua teaches us how to subdivide land; the Book of Numbers addresses city-planning issues; Nehemiah deals with mortgages and collateral; Job mentions expropriation; and the Book of Daniel describes the real estate developer.

But different cultures have different concepts of land use and ownership. For instance, unlike purchase or lease, consent to use something (such as land or water) and benefit from it is called usufruct (from the Latin *ususfructus,* from *usus et fructus,* "use and enjoyment"). Usufruct gives persons or groups the right to use a resource such as land for a specific purpose, usually related to farming, harvesting trees or fishing and hunting. An example today would be a landowner giving a farmer a right to harvest hay in exchange for a bale or two or a piece of the profits. Unlike fee simple ownership, usufruct is closer to the way North American Aboriginal peoples use, share and give rights to their traditional territories. Although no longer in common use in real estate development, the term *usufruct* is in use today among the Native communities of North America. They resent, however, the white man taking their land away from them and then giving them the right to use it.

Giving someone the right to use land for a specific purpose like farming is a form of usufruct.

### Ancient Arguments for and against Private Ownership

Arguments as to the merits of public and private ownership of land took place in Greece as early as the fourth century BCE. The first writers on economics that we have records of were concerned with land. They understood the importance of land as a factor in agricultural production and devoted their attention principally to the question of ownership. Although Plato (ca. 428–348 BCE) argued for public ownership of land, Aristotle (384–322 BCE) argued for private ownership.

In *The Republic* (380 BCE), Plato called for common ownership of land by the state as a means of removing sources of discontent. But sometime later in *Laws,* his last and longest discourse, written circa 360 BCE, he advocated for private ownership of land and houses because he believed that the people were not capable of managing their affairs in common. The way some strata and co-ownership organizations function today would support Plato's theory.

Aristotle, on the other hand, did not favor common ownership. To him, private ownership, through which an individual was assured the result of his labor, seemed more likely to elicit greater commitment and more conscientious attention to obligations. He did, however, advocate restrictions on the accumulation of property, mainly through limitations on inheritance. Aristotle explains this in his *Politics*:

> That which is common to the greatest number has the least care bestowed upon it. Everyone thinks chiefly of his own, hardly at all of the common interest; and only when he is himself concerned as an individual. For besides other considerations, everybody is more inclined to neglect the duty which he expects another to fulfil.

Aristotle draws a parallel between the love in private relationships and the love of property. He argues that we have a personal relationship with our property and a desire to be protective of it, something we feel much less in a communal setting. Robert Nisbet, a contemporary social theorist, sums up Aristotle's view as "property that is the possession of all is nobody's."[1] Aristotle, nonetheless, agreed with Plato that extreme inequalities were latent in private ownership, and that it would lead to social strife. Both Plato and Aristotle were right. Social strife did occur, but it also led to the development of a great deal of real estate.

In his book *Property and Freedom,* Richard Pipes states that the history of all societies, from the primitive to the most advanced, reveals the universality of real property claims and the failure of every attempt to form a "property-less" society, either voluntarily or by force.[2] This failure is especially noted in the attempts to create utopian communities (see chapter 12).

## Legal Ownership and Expropriation

Since land is the key prerequisite for real estate development, there are only two ways to acquire it: by force or by law. But possessing land by force—whether it is Alexander conquering all of Macedonia (see chapter 4), Genghis Khan capturing all of Asia, or more contemporary versions of land grabs that we are aware of (see sidebar page 32)—never leads to "certainty."

Possessing land by law—that is, securing title through purchase, lease, expropriation or inheritance—provides greater security than taking land by force. One of the things that concerned the estate holders who were granted previously held Church property by Henry VIII circa 1539 was the fear that the taking of it was illegal. At the time, they did not feel they had secure title to the land and were afraid that it might revert to the Catholic Church. They lacked certainty.

1   Robert Nisbet, *The Social Philosophers: Community and Conflict in Western Thought* (New York: Thomas Y. Crowell, 1973), 395.

2   Richard Pipes, *Property and Freedom* (New York: Vintage Books, 2000).

## LAND GRABS IN AMERICA

The Dutch in 1648 really pulled one over on Native Americans by purchasing the entire island of Manhattan for the measly equivalent of $24 in beads and trinkets. If that wasn't a land grab, even if it is a myth, I don't know what is.

However, the most extensive real estate land grabs, well in excess of the Dutch acquisition of Manhattan Island or Henry VIII's Dissolution of the Monasteries in the 1500s (see chapter 7), occurred in North America in the 1700s prior to the American Revolution. Millions of acres were secured through dubious transactions, with title and ownership transferred from indigenous nations despite the Crown barring such transactions.

Land speculators did not heed restrictions from Britain against acquiring "Indian Lands." The most noted of these speculators were well-known leaders of the Revolution, including George Washington, Thomas Jefferson, Benjamin Franklin and Patrick Henry. Later, Thomas Jefferson in his waning years lamented the role he had played in these dubious transactions.

Patrick Henry was one of the most violent of the Founding Fathers in his denunciation of Britain's tyranny with respect to their restrictions on land acquisitions. Jefferson described Henry as being insatiable in regard to money. Henry's participation in Georgia's Yazoo land fraud of 1785 would bear this out.

Strong evidence indicates that the American Revolution may not have been fought over tea or taxation without representation, but over land. The need to get out from under the yoke of Great Britain and to grab land was paramount.

The uncertainty of title was earlier made clear when the Normans conquered England in 1066. Until that moment, estate law in England was simple: in the feudal land system, land was the sole form of wealth, and if you possessed it, you owned it. But William I, the conquering Norman, decreed that he owned all the land of England by right of conquest. Only huge land grants given by the new king to his officers or supporters replaced privately held land. And tenure then became the king's means to control and administer his land. The assignee of the land worked out a deal to hold his land via tenure on direct approval from the king.

These so-called tenants-in-chief in turn could sublet their land to others. Tenures of various duration were called estates, and a fee simple estate, the most widespread form of tenure, allowed the tenant to sell, convey by will or transfer to his heir the land under his control. The English jurist William Blackstone (1723–80) defined *fee simple* as the stake in land that a person has when the lands are given to him and his heirs absolutely, without any end or limit.

Today in most countries, land is acquired legally, though it may come with limited rights (zoning, restricted covenants, and so on). Under current laws in democratic nations, one cannot lose the rights to that property without due process of law and/or proper compensation. This has not been the case under corrupt regimes or dictatorships. For example, real estate developers who thought they bought property legally after Daniel Ortega was ousted from Nicaragua found out, after he returned to power ten years later, that they did not own it any more. Their properties, with all the improvements made on them in the interim, were returned to their original owners or to others. These developers or property owners had their land expropriated without due process or compensation—and not for public purposes. This was in conflict with the precedent of centuries.

## THE NAPOLEONIC CODE

Property rights were democratically protected in France in 1804 under the Napoleonic Code. The code, among other things, forbade privileges based on birth, allowed freedom of religion and specified that government jobs go to the most qualified. With its stress on clearly written and accessible law, the code was a major step in establishing the rule of law. But Napoleon III modified the code, permitting the expropriation of vast parts of Paris to permit the redevelopment of that city by the emperor and his planner Baron Haussmann (see chapter 11). Today in North America, the Napoleonic Code still operates in Quebec and Louisiana.

As early as 2100 BCE, the Third Dynasty of Ur established a functioning legal system, with laws pertaining to property expressed in the Code of Ur-Nammu (see next chapter). Laws relating to property later appeared in the Code of Hammurabi (see page 40) and then the Old Testament. Roman lawmakers were the first to formulate the concept of absolute private ownership, which they called "dominion." Dominion applied to real estate and to slaves. Roman law stipulated how property was acquired, lost, transferred and sold, but it said nothing about the concept of eminent domain. In modern times and until recently, the use of eminent domain for the purposes of expropriation in the United States, Canada and most of Europe has been limited by law so that it could only be used for the public good. This was generally defined as projects such as roads, transportation and utility corridors, or providing land for public institutions (such as schools and hospitals).

Such expropriation of land took place in Paris during the time of Napoleon III (see sidebar and chapter 11). Another example is the acquiring of lands for New York's Central Park in the early 1850s, which was the first time the law of eminent domain (from the Latin *dominium eminens,* "supreme lordship") was applied in the United States. During the postwar years, slum clearances and the building of housing projects were also considered in the public good, and extensive expropriation and demolition took place under the concept of urban renewal.

In 2005, the U.S. Supreme Court ruled in favor of the city of New London, Connecticut, by determining that economic development was a public good with respect to the "taking of land," thereby expanding the definition

of what was allowable and permitting the expropriation of private property for the construction of a private commercial shopping center. This ruling overturned years of precedent regarding the terms under which the public sector could exercise the power of eminent domain under the Fifth Amendment. Although a U.S. ruling, it has already had an impact on other jurisdictions.

At the start of the nineteenth century, with laws in place to protect property rights, greater investment in real estate development was possible. But most real estate development, at least until that time, was realized largely by the elite: the Church, royalty, the wealthy patron, the architect-builder or the industrial tycoon. Over time, however, free enterprise, democratic institutions, the availability of capital and credit, and the ability to purchase land or receive land grants (through extensive homesteading in the United States and Canada) meant real estate development was no longer limited to those with money or to the aristocracy. Now anyone with a wheelbarrow and a brother-in-law could become a builder and in many cases become a real estate developer, and many of these "anyones" did.

In addition to the establishment of laws, other developments and historical events advanced real estate; they included the establishment of regulated banking beginning in the seventeenth century, the free flow of international currency beginning in the eighteenth century, the Industrial Revolution of the nineteenth century and the increasing importance of global trade, continuing and expanding from the sixteenth to the twenty-first century. Preparations for many of these events began with the establishment of the earliest cities—magnets for people, buildings and early real estate developers.

# 03

# The City of Ur
# and the Ziggurat

*My wife and I travel often to California, but we had never
visited the state capital of Sacramento. We were intrigued
by stories of relics of Chinese junks found in the Sacramento
River—and also of a Chinese colony predating the arrival
of Francis Drake on the west coast of America or even of
Columbus on the east coast. We had no idea that a city that
appeared so far inland was an important port, connected to
the sea via the Sacramento River.*

*On a recent trip, we drove to Sacramento to explore. When
we arrived, we were struck by the sight of an office building in
the form of a ziggurat on the edge of the river. The ziggurat
(a truncated pyramid) is a very unusual ancient building form
rarely seen today and which dates back to early placemaking
and the cities of Uruk and Ur.*

1    *The Epic of Gilgamesh*, Tablet I, trans. Maureen Gallery Kovacs (Academy for Ancient Texts), http://www.ancienttexts. org/library/mesopotamian/ gilgamesh/tab1.htm.

ONE OF THE FIRST real cities in the world was Uruk (pronounced OO-rook), situated east of the Euphrates River in Mesopotamia, in modern-day Iraq. It later became the city of Sumer and then Babylonia. The city of Uruk is considered not only the first city built, about 4000 BCE, but also the first to introduce the art of building out of stone and the form of the ziggurat. In 2900 BCE, the Sumerians were at the height of their power, and Uruk was at that time the largest city in the world, housing some sixty thousand citizens within its walls. Gilgamesh, its fabled Sumerian king, ruled in the twenty-seventh century BCE, his life transformed in literature into the demigod who protects his people at all costs. The tale of his achievements, recorded in Tablet XI of *The Epic of Gilgamesh* (see sidebar), opens with a description of the city of Uruk—its walls, streets, markets, temples and gardens:

> Look at its wall which gleams like copper,
>
> inspect its inner wall, the likes of which no one can equal!
>
> Take hold of the threshold stone—it dates from ancient times!
>
> Go close to the Nanna Temple, the residence of Ishtar,
>
> such as no later king or man ever equaled!
>
> Go up on the wall of Uruk and walk around,
>
> examine its foundation, inspect its brickwork thoroughly.
>
> Is not the core of the brick structure made of kiln-fired brick,
>
> and did not the Seven Sages themselves lay out its plans? [1]

A number of other firsts, besides being recognized as one of the first true cities, created Uruk's renown. It is said to be the place where writing originated, and it featured the first architectural work in stone, leading to the building of large stone structures. It was also the first city to develop the cylinder seal, which the ancient Mesopotamians used to designate personal property or as a signature on documents. The seal was a critical step in acknowledging individual identity. In addition, Uruk originated the ziggurat, a terraced but low-stepped pyramid of successively receding stories or levels.

Ancient cities such as Uruk and Ur were only partially planned. Uruk began around a temple, initially a small room that soon became a massive multi-acre temple complex designed to celebrate a sacred place. Uruk's expansion into a city inaugurated the concept of real estate development, and Gilgamesh could be considered the first real estate developer and placemaker. Uruk thrived as the center of power for over two thousand years but began to decline in roughly 2000 BCE because of other cities being built closer to the Persian Gulf, a location more advantageous for trade. Following its demise, it lay abandoned and buried until excavated between 1850 and 1854 CE by William Loftus for the British Museum. With its decline, the center

## THE EPIC OF GILGAMESH

Discovered by the archaeologist Hormuzd Rassam in 1853, *The Epic of Gilgamesh* is now widely known. Twelve stone tablets form the work, written from 2100 to 1200 BCE. George Smith published the first modern translation of the epic in the early 1870s. Elements of *The Epic of Gilgamesh*, including themes, plot and characters, find parallels in the Hebrew Bible and include the Garden of Eden and the narrative of the flood in Genesis.

Predating Homer's *Iliad* and *Odyssey* by 1,500 years, this Sumerian/Babylonian work stands as the oldest piece of epic Western literature. Gilgamesh is the mythical ruler of Uruk presented in the epic. His father was the priest-king Lugalbanda, and his mother the goddess Ninsun (the Holy Mother and Great Queen). Accordingly, Gilgamesh was thought otherworldly and said to have lived 126 years and to have possessed superhuman strength.

of power moved to Ur, in southern Iraq in ancient Mesopotamia, ruled by King Ur-Nammu, who built the temple of Ur and the city of Ur surrounding it, the temple in the form of a ziggurat.

The Ziggurat of Ur is 200 by 150 feet (60 by 45 m) at the base and stands over 100 feet (30 m) high on land between the Tigris and Euphrates Rivers. This truncated pyramid ended up being converted from a temple into the administrative center of the city.

The establishment of the cities of Uruk and Ur happened during the so-called Neolithic Revolution, which transformed small and mobile groups of hunter-gatherers into sedentary societies rooted in built-up villages and towns. These developments provided the basis for concentrated, higher-density settlements, with specialized and complex divisions of labor, as well as the creation of art, architecture and culture. These early settlements also instituted centralized administrative and political organizations and laws.

Sumerian and Ur real estate developments were not limited to the ziggurat form: they included the invention of urban planning and the courtyard house. Without formally trained architects, scribes managed to draft plans and oversee construction for housing for members of the government and nobility, who became, as did Gilgamesh in Uruk, Ur's real estate developers and placemakers.

Lacking forests and quarries, Sumerians used mostly sunbaked clay bricks as their building material (not unlike the adobe later used by Hopi Natives for their pueblos). Over time, Sumerian structures deteriorated; consequently, there are few surviving built traces of their civilization. But the Code of Ur-Nammu, with its laws about the possession, transfer and use of property, remained, shaping both the Code of Hammurabi, one of the earliest sets of laws (created ca. 1780 BCE), and those laws found in the Old Testament. In fact, the Old Testament mentions

The Ziggurat of Ur, in one of the earliest known cities, started out to celebrate a sacred place and ended up being the administrative center of the city. Ziggurats built by other cultures include this Mayan temple in Chichén Itzá, Yucatán (center), and the contemporary Great Stupa of Universal Compassion, a Buddhist temple in Australia (bottom).

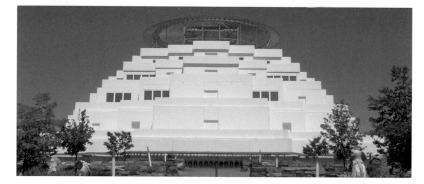

## THE ZIGGURAT AS
## A BUILDING FORM

Why is the ziggurat form (a truncated pyramid) not an efficient form for commercial office buildings? The efficiency of commercial office buildings is measured by both tenants and building owners as the ratio of core facilities to floor area. The core normally includes the toilets, elevator shafts, fire stairs, mechanical rooms and shafts and, on multi-tenanted floors, the public corridors as well. Another important measure is the distance between inner offices and the window wall.

If you envision the ziggurat shape, with very large floors at the base and very tiny floors at the top, you can immediately see that it would have a very high ratio of core facilities on the upper floors and a great distance to the window wall on the lower floors.

In addition to these marketing and efficiency factors, it is a given that vertical services increase in size and cost every six floors in height. This means that as one builds up the ziggurat, the cost of reaching the upper floors with mechanical services, stairs and elevators becomes more expensive for each buildable foot of rentable area.

And this is why the ziggurat, as interesting and historic a shape as it may be, and as applicable as it may be for the construction of a sacred place in Ur or a single tenant seeking an identity symbol in Sacramento, is not an efficient building form for commercial office buildings or, for that matter, for apartment complexes.

However, it is a logical form when one is building with stone and wanting to celebrate a sacred place, as did the Sumerians, Egyptians and Mayans.

Ur four times, and the city is thought to be the birthplace of Abraham. The laws of Ur-Nammu additionally made it a requirement to record real estate transactions, and from those records it is possible to discover the pattern of urban growth, density and property values. Ur, with a population of approximately sixty-five thousand, was the largest city in the world from 2030 to 1980 BCE, later to be eclipsed by Alexandria, discussed in the next chapter.

# 04

# Alexandria
# in Ancient Egypt

*When I was studying architecture at university, I was in the habit
of wandering through used bookstores in search of interesting
works on the subject so that I could impress my professors with
new knowledge and seek ideas for upcoming projects. At least the
knowledge and ideas were new to me. One day, I came across a
wonderful little book written by Trystan Edwards. This ex-military
man who became a pioneer architect and town planner was much
criticized for proposing the densification of small English towns
with the construction of town houses, an idea currently promoted
by Prince Charles. A man of mercurial temperament and fine
taste, Edwards was contemptuous of the monumental skyscraper,
but he did acknowledge that a fine building is worthy of individual
attention.*

*His book I picked up, published in 1924, was entitled* Good and
Bad Manners in Architecture.[1] *In it Edwards attempts to show
how buildings may pay due respect to each other and live sociably
together. But he also points out that you can discern the vocation
of a city by its tallest building. It was an interesting observation
that applies to ancient Alexandria and to more contemporary
cities as well.*

1    Trystan Edwards, *Good and Bad Manners in Architecture: An Essay on the
Social Aspects of Civic Design* (London: Philip Allan, 1924).

THE MEDITERRANEAN PORT CITY of Alexandria, Egypt, was founded and planned by Alexander III of Macedonia, also known as Alexander the Great, Aristotle's most famous pupil. Born in Pella in 356 BCE to Philip II, then king of Macedonia, and one of his eight wives, Olympias, Alexander rose to be an intellectual and a leader. His parents had great ambitions for him, partly imbued by the gods. Philip II, a boyhood friend of Aristotle, decided to send Alexander to study with the philosopher and scientist. The education Alexander received from Aristotle taught him ethics, politics and strategy, all to assist him in his later accomplishments.

Alexander, sent by his father, Philip II, to study with the great Greek philosopher Aristotle, received an exceptional education.

Soon, Alexander's parents felt Macedonia was too small for him to rule and encouraged him to believe it was his destiny to conquer the Persian Empire. He believed them and went on to do just that, establishing one of the greatest empires of the ancient world. His conquests launched the beginnings of the Hellenistic period. But although most know Alexander as a great military leader, few know that he was one of the first recorded real estate developers of cities, including the town in Egypt that now bears his name. It was designed and planned by the young Greek architect Dinocrates.

In trying to secure a commission from Alexander, Dinocrates had difficulty getting an audience with the emperor. After being rebuffed by Alexander's officers a number of times, he hatched a scheme to assure their meeting. Dinocrates went to the agora, secured props, stripped to the waist, oiled his body, placed a chaplet of poplar leaves as a crown on his head, threw a lion's skin over his left shoulder, grasped a club in his right hand and strode off to the place where Alexander was administering justice.

His appearance had the desired sensational effect. The people at the court, the officers and soldiers, were startled. Was this a ghost or a man? Alexander was curious and when told there must be a god among them, he was anxious to see the apparition. He ordered the crowd to stand back so that the odd figure could draw near.

Announcing himself to the emperor, he said, "I am Dinocrates of Rhodes, the architect, and I propose to design for the emperor a city worthy of royal renown." He then described how he would carve Mount Athos into a statue of a man holding a spacious city in his left hand and, in his right, a huge cup into which would be collected all the streams of the mountain, to then be poured into the sea. But Alexander had visited Mount

Athos; he was familiar with the area and knew that there was insufficient arable land and water on the mountain to sustain such a city. He explained to the young architect that the first rule of real estate development was *"Topothesia, topothesia, topothesia!"*—"Location, location, location!"

Although critical of Dinocrates's performance, Alexander nonetheless admired his ambition and imagination, and invited him to join him in Egypt to be his architect. Plutarch, in his life of Alexander, writes of their voyage when they arrived at the island of Pharos in 332 BCE:

> As soon as he [Alexander] saw the commodious situation of the place, it being a long neck of land, stretching like an isthmus between large lagoons and shallow waters on one side and the sea on the other, the latter at the end of it making a spacious harbour, he… ordered the plan of a city to be drawn out answerable to the place. To do which, for want of chalk, and the soil being black, they laid out their lines in flour.[2]

Dinocrates conceived the design of the new city and its harbor by forming a semicircular figure on the ground and drawing into the middle of the circumference equal straight lines from end to end, thus giving it something of the form of a cloak. Alexander was pleased with this design, but as he was admiring it, a flock of black birds descended upon the site and devoured every morsel of flour used by Dinocrates to lay out the design on the black soil. Dinocrates took this as an evil omen and urged Alexander to abandon the project.

But Alexander was resolute in his designs and firm in his opinions. He had a passion for surmounting difficulties and building things. In other words, he had the ideal characteristics for being a real estate developer.

2   Plutarch, [*Life* of] *Alexander*, trans. John Dryden, para. 41 (Internet Classics Archive), http://classics.mit.edu/Plutarch/alexandr.html.

Alexander and his young Greek
architect Dinocrates plan the
port city of Alexandria.

Alexander commanded Dinocrates to tell the workers to
continue despite the omen of the birds, for he was determined
to build a splendid city that would bear his name, calling it
Alexandria. Plutarch writes that Alexander predicted, "The City
will be very rich and will nourish men of all races." And it
did. Alexandria was not only the center of Hellenism but also
became home to the largest Jewish community in the world at
that time. It was here that the Septuagint, a Greek translation
of the Hebrew Bible, was produced, its text populated with
references to real estate.

The speed of construction and success of the city was possible because Alexander had control over a large piece of property, had access to extensive finances, and was able to avoid laws, obligations or bad omens (like a flock of black birds). Alexandria became a beautiful city, meticulous in its order and sense of balance. Five hundred years later, the Greek writer Achilles Tatius described Alexandria in Book v of his ancient romance *Leucippe and Clitophon* in this fashion:

> Two things struck me as especially strange and extraordinary —it was impossible to decide which was the greatest, the size of the place or its beauty, the city itself or its inhabitants; for the former was larger than a continent, the latter outnumbered a whole nation. Looking at the city, I doubted whether any race of men could ever fill it; looking at the inhabitants, I wondered whether any city could ever be found large enough to hold them all. The balance seemed exactly even.[3]

He goes on to describe a procession of torches after sunset during "the sacred festival of the great god whom the Greeks call Zeus, the Egyptians Serapis... It was the greatest spectacle I ever beheld... I thought that on that occasion the city vied with the sky for beauty."[4]

Alexander himself never saw his beautiful city completed. He died at the age of thirty-two and before he had time to put into place any plans for succession. As a result of this oversight, fighting broke out among his four generals and they decided to divide up the empire, with Ptolemy taking over the island of Rhodes and Egypt, becoming the new ruler of the latter. Together, he and Dinocrates finished Alexander's real estate development project—building the city of Alexandria. But a city needs more than buildings; it needs a vocation. For Alexandria, that purpose was maritime commerce.

3   Achilles Tatius, *Leucippe and Clitophon*, trans. S. Gaselee, Loeb Classical Library 45 (Cambridge, MA: Harvard University Press, 1969), 237–38.

4   Ibid., 238.

## THE MARINE BUILDING

For many years the tallest building in Vancouver, British Columbia, was the Marine Building, a twenty-two-story art deco masterpiece that opened in October 1930. Designed by the Vancouver architectural firm of McCarter Nairne, the building was inspired by New York City's Chrysler Building.

The idea for the building came to its developer, Lieutenant-Commander J.W. Hobbs, when he realized that after the opening of the Panama Canal in 1914, Vancouver could become a major port. Marine-related businesses, in addition to customs and immigration offices, would need office space near the waterfront. By virtue of its name, height, decor and tenants, the Marine Building declared to the world the importance of Vancouver as a west coast maritime center. Today, Vancouver's tallest building is the sixty-one-story Shangri-La Hotel, built in 2008.

Top: The Marine Building when it opened in 1930 was Vancouver's tallest building and proclaimed the city to be an important port.

Bottom: When the sixty-one-story Shangri-La Hotel and apartment building opened in 2008, it became Vancouver's tallest, indicating that the city, as a port, had changed its vocation.

Under Ptolemy, Rhodes and Egypt controlled most of the trade in the Mediterranean. Alexandria thrived as a port because of its location and quickly became the center of commerce of the Greco-Roman world. Because of its great library, with its immense repository of books, it also became one of the most important centers of learning in the world, especially in the fields of mathematics, history and literature. As the city grew, it needed a way to guide ships through the harbor. Ptolemy also felt it needed something that would stand for its riches and greatness. In addition to its name, it needed a symbol of identity.

In 290 BCE, Ptolemy began to build the Pharos or lighthouse, which, prior to his death, Alexander had ordered constructed after imagining it in a dream. Designed by another Greek architect, Sostratus of Cnidus, the Pharos (actually built on the island of Pharos at the head of the harbor) was completed twenty years later—the first lighthouse in the world and at 450 feet (137 m), the tallest building on Earth, on a par with the Great Pyramid of Giza, in Egypt. The Pharos was later considered to be one of the Seven Wonders of the Ancient World. It was destroyed by an earthquake in the fourteenth century.

The Pharos, the tallest building in the world at the time, declared Alexandria to be a great port.

Proud of his work, Sostratus wanted to carve his name into the base of the completed lighthouse. Ptolemy refused this request, ordering that only his own name appear. But Sostratus found a way to outsmart him. At the base of the Pharos, Sostratus carved a message containing his own name. He then covered the message with a weak form of plaster and carved Ptolemy's name over his own. After many years, the plaster bearing Ptolemy's name chipped away to reveal that of Sostratus, the true architect of the lighthouse. Real estate development as an expression of personal accomplishment had begun.

The Romans, as well as the Greeks, also soon learned the importance of naming buildings, as the next chapter illustrates.

**05**

# Rome: Republic and Empire

Emperor Augustus saw to
the renewal and expansion
of Rome in the first century.

*I met the Vancouver restaurateur Umberto Menghi when I
first came to Vancouver in the early 1970s, at the same time
the famous Italian tenor Luciano Pavarotti was giving a
concert. Umberto could not attend because he was preparing
a post-concert supper for the great tenor and his guests.
Through friends, it was arranged that I would use Umberto's
concert ticket and accompany his wife to the concert.
Although this was early in Pavarotti's career, the Orpheum
theater was jammed; to accommodate the overflow, hundreds
of seats had been placed onstage. Umberto told me later that
evening that every tile setter in town was in the audience.*

*What makes Italians such great tile and marble setters and
great pourers of concrete? Well, their proficiency goes back to
the days of Augustus of Rome.*

THE ROMAN REPUBLIC—or *Res Publica Romana*—followed the Greek classical period. It began with the overthrow of the Roman monarchy, around 509 BCE. A government headed by two consuls replaced the monarchy. These consuls were elected annually by the citizens and advised by a senate: in short, a republic. The Roman Republic was marked by extensive building projects, both civic and military, throughout the empire, the developer being essentially the government, which needed to both expand and protect its territory.

Conquests and alliances led to growth of the empire, but each step forward required more buildings. Advances in civil engineering and technology permitted Roman buildings to be built on a grand scale. Many of these structures still stand today, among them amphitheaters, baths, aqueducts, civic forums and even the Colosseum.

Life in the Roman Republic and later the Roman Empire revolved around Rome, the administrative and cultural center. Its famed Seven Hills meant development problems that often could be solved only by private rather than government means. Increasingly, private fortunes underwrote the building boom for private residences on land that constantly offered topographic challenges.

It was Emperor Augustus who saw to the renewal and expansion of Rome in the first century CE, becoming in effect the first Roman real estate developer. He accomplished this not only through building but also through regulation and law. He established building codes; he reorganized the city into neighborhoods administered at the local level, with police and firefighting services; and he also instituted programs promoting building

Augustus found Rome a city of bricks and left it a city of marble.

Palatine Hill, Augustus's great
real estate development in Rome,
included his temple to Apollo.

maintenance, stronger construction materials and safe streets. These activities resulted in the fabrication of an imperial urban image, the product of building on a massive scale, with projects such as the Parthenon and the Forum. The imperial appropriation of public space refashioned the scale and image of the city. Memorably, for Augustan Rome, the city was being redesigned in the conceptual and physical image of one man.

In short, Augustus (63 BCE–14 CE), originally named Octavius, forged the transition from the Roman Republic to the Roman Empire, which meant recasting the Republican city on the Tiber River into an imperial capital. Through new construction, physical redevelopment and even housing, he managed to convey the importance of Rome as the seat of a great state *and* the home of a singular leader. The city became a tool for legitimizing the wielding of imperial and personal might. Athens initially overshadowed Republican Rome, but Augustus turned that over through his building program, infrastructure and power, in the process becoming a great placemaker, in certain ways the ultimate developer. His display of classical Grecian art in sacred settings visually reminded the populace of the dignity they must display in the first city of the empire.

As a result, Rome became the administrative and government center of the empire, as well as a sacred place. Romans quickly became experienced readers of nonverbal texts: they understood what grandeur in art and architecture meant as symbols of power. One did not have to be an *erudito* (an erudite scholar) to grasp the symbolism and history expressed in Rome. Everyone understood that to walk through safe streets meant a stable government, while monuments represented individual heroism and national power. By contrast, derelict buildings meant municipal poverty and disregard, something Napoleon III would later understand (see chapter 11). Such a complex union of dissimilar individuals oddly benefiting from density and power made Rome a living space composed of urban spaces, not individual buildings. An educated Roman senator and a slave might share the same streetscape. Ritual events such as parades linked disparate sections of the city.

To develop the city, however, required the patronage, as well as the money, of the emperor. Augustus had the ability to offer both, and he understood, as Alexander did, and as Donald

Classical Greek statuary helped to enhance the city of Rome, where grandeur in art and architecture was symbolic of imperial power.

Trump and other developers would later learn, that to attach your name to a building was critical. Placing one's name on a structure empowered patrons (or the emperor) with *genius loci,* a powerful association with the spirit of a place within the city. Preceding Augustus, Caesar took advantage of this concept by creating and naming the Forum Julium (this new public space supplemented the overcrowded Forum Romanum); the Basilica Julia (a large public building used for official business and meetings favored by the Roman public; it was originally in the Forum Romanum); the Curia Julia (the building of the Roman senate, where senators and the emperor met); and the Stadium Caesaris (a large stadium where races were run).

Yet, even while Augustus tried to promote private responsibility for urban development, he realized the importance of public works and the need to underwrite the building and repair of roads. When the senate would not support him, he personally underwrote the maintenance of highways around Rome. He also took over care of the Tiber, the main commercial artery. He had the riverbed cleared of rubbish and removed structures that narrowed the river's passage. He also instituted games, theatrical performances and religious ceremonies that—directly or not—celebrated his achievements, in this way renewing a sense of community and support.

Augustus was, however, cautious. He restricted the size of his forum for fear of being seen to dispossess those living nearby. He wanted to ensure balance between civic space and private activity, diminishing the divide between the elite and the citizens. To this end he began an immense program of public works, supervised not by a central board but by separate boards responsible for individual areas. This reorganization of social space encouraged the shift of public works from private control to the imperial administration.

## Living It Up: High-Rise Apartments in Early Rome

At its peak, Rome was estimated to have a population of one million, not exceeded by any other major European city until 1900. But the one million were packed within 1,700 acres (690 ha). The city boasted several theaters, gymnasiums and many taverns, baths, brothels and apartment buildings (see sidebar page 62). Like most Roman cities, it had a forum and temple as well. It constantly competed, implicitly, with Athens: in the center of the city was a museum of Greek sculpture. Architecture as a private space became so important at this time that embossed on the coins of Emperor Augustus was his front door, flanked by two laurel trees sacred to Apollo.

Under Rome's control, residential architecture throughout the territory ranged from modest houses to country villas. In Rome itself, housing encompassed barely livable private spaces, as well as dwellings on the elegant Palatine Hill, from which the word *palace* is derived.

Multistory buildings provided an answer to the growing overpopulation, satisfying the remark of Vitruvius. In about 1 CE he wrote in his *Ten Books of Architecture* that the size of Rome "makes it needful to have a vast number of habitations, and, as the area is not sufficient to contain them all on the ground floor, the nature of the case compels us to raise them in the air."[1] The vast majority of residents lived in the city center, packed into large high-rise apartment blocks that were often no more than squalid firetraps. These were called *insulae* (islands), built six or more stories high out of baked bricks, with the owner of the tenement living on the lower two floors. Lists of the city wards from the fourth century indicate there were only 1,800 private homes versus 46,600 blocks of flats. And as more and more apartments were built, their height increased.

1    Vitruvius quoted in William Stearns Davis, *A Day in Old Rome: A Picture of Roman Life* (New York: Biblio & Tannen, 1967), 35.

2    Plutarch, [*Life of*] *Crassus*, trans. John Dryden (Internet Classics Archive), para. 2, http://classics.mit.edu/Plutarch/crassus.html.

One of the earlier private property owners, and perhaps the first recorded slumlord, Marcus Licinius Crassus (also a general and politician), organized the first fire brigade in Rome—but it only fought fires that threatened buildings he owned. He also is reported to have profited from fires. According to John Dryden's translation of Plutarch's life of *Crassus*, "Observing how extremely subject the city was to fire and falling down of houses, by reason of their height and their standing so near together,... [Crassus] made it his practice to buy houses that were on fire, and those in the neighborhood, which, in the immediate danger and uncertainty the proprietors were willing to part with for little or nothing, so that the greatest part of Rome, at one time or other, came into his hands."[2]

Many Romans lived in the center of the city in "insulae" made of brick and timber, some rising to twelve stories.

## DID ROMANS
## LIVE IN CONDOS?

Although the word *condominium* stems from the Latin *com*, "together," and *dominium*, "right of ownership," that's about as far as the connection goes.[3] In ancient Rome, there was no condominium ownership, which if it existed would have been against Roman law. The term *condominium* was coined by the Germans in 1700 and applied until the nineteenth century to joint sovereignty over land and not co-ownership of buildings.

It is this use of the term in the 1700s that was applied to the co-sovereignty of an island in the middle of a river between France and Spain. And today professors in Canada and Denmark are suggesting the concept be applied to solving the ownership controversy over Hans Island, which lies between Greenland and Ellesmere Island.

The French adopted the word *condominium* for co-ownership or horizontal ownership of apartments in the mid-1800s, which made possible the financing of new apartment buildings as part of Haussmann's rebuilding of Paris (see chapter 11).

Although cooperative apartments were built in North America as early as 1900, condominium legislation did not appear in the United States until 1962, after it was instituted in Puerto Rico in 1958. Canada did not get its first registered condo until 1967. In Quebec, condominium ownership is known as "co-ownership" and in British Columbia as "strata title."

3   The myth of condominium ownership in Roman times was debunked in "Comments on the Historiography of Condominium: The Myth of Roman Origin," by Robert G. Natelson of the University of Montana School of Law. His article appeared in the *Oklahoma City University Law Review* 12, no. 1 (Spring 1987): 17–58, http://scholarship.law. umt.edu/cgi/viewcontent. cgi?article=1042&context= faculty_lawreviews.

More high-rise apartment buildings started to appear in response to the growing population. Some reached up to ten or more stories, with one reportedly having two hundred stairs. Because poorly built high-rise apartment buildings were collapsing, several Roman emperors, beginning with Augustus, set height limits of 60 to 75 feet (20 to 25 m) for multistory buildings. But builders often ignored these limits, despite the likelihood of taller buildings falling down. Surviving documents indicate that seven-story buildings existed even in provincial towns such as Pompeii or Herculaneum.

### Houses, Villas and Concrete Innovations

The rich in Rome surprisingly did not live in separate enclaves. Their houses were intended to be accessible and visible. The atrium functioned as a reception hall, a space where the leader of the household met with clients every morning. These clients ranged from wealthy friends to poor dependents who received charity. The atrium was also the location for family religious rites, and often housed a shrine and images of deceased family members.

Busy public roads were the general location of the homes of the wealthy, with ground-level spaces facing the street often rented out as shops. Town houses typically enclosed a peristyle garden (a columned porch or open colonnade in a building surrounding a courtyard), including a kitchen garden that brought a bit of nature within the walls.

The villa, by contrast with these densely surrounded urban dwellings, was an escape from the activity of the city, ideally commanding a view or vista. It might be located on a working estate or in a resort town situated on the seacoast. Pompeii and Herculaneum were favorites.

A photo of the Getty Villa, which recreates an ancient Roman country house and exhibits over 1,200 antiquities from the ancient Greek and Roman worlds.

Besides apartment high-rises, public buildings and private homes, the Romans constructed numerous aqueducts, reflecting the administrative importance placed on ensuring a water supply. They knew, as did Alexander, that to sustain a community, one needed water. The Pont du Gard aqueduct, crossing the Gardon River in southern France, still stands, thanks to the secret of Roman concrete. This secret, which has literally lasted centuries, has remained a riddle: even after more than two thousand years, some Roman structures still stand magnificently.

The Romans did not invent lime mortar, but they were the first to see its possibilities to produce concrete. Concrete rubble had been used as a filler material, but Roman architects soon realized that the material could support great weight and could, therefore, work to help span space and create new building opportunities. It was reliable and would harden into an almost impregnable material. Its thick consistency meant it had to be laid, not poured like modern concrete. The third century BCE saw its first use; its first use in Rome, in a storehouse, is thought to be in the second century BCE.

In addition to the structural possibilities, concrete was cheaper than solid stone and could be given a more attractive facade using stucco, marble veneer or another inexpensive material, often fired brick or terra-cotta. Sun-dried mud bricks had been used for centuries and continued to be used for more modest projects up to the first century CE. However, fired bricks had proven durability and could be carved like stone to resemble such typical architectural features as capitals and dentils.

Besides their concrete innovations, the Romans invented double glazing, which they used in the construction of public baths. Elite housing in cooler climates might also feature a hypocaust, a form of central heating under the floor relying on circulating hot air (*hypo* means "under"; *caust* means "burnt"). Building materials from foreign lands, especially marble, used throughout Rome, expressed Roman control of distant territories, underlining Rome as the capital of the empire. Roman architecture also favored the Corinthian order (the third of the classical orders, following Doric and Ionic). Used as ornament for columns, the form had its roots in Corinth and was formerly used to underscore sacred space in Greece. In adopting this style, and in other ways, Augustus effectively made Rome a sacred space, all the more so when he displayed masterpieces from classical Greek sanctuaries.

Over the centuries, popes replaced emperors as developers, and by the early eighteenth century initiated ambitious building plans. Clement XII, for example, built new streets (a road from the Trevi Fountain to the Quirinal Hill), created the Capitoline Museum, restored the Arch of Constantine and constructed a new wing of the Vatican Library. During this period, Rome resembled a giant construction site, with laborers and masons straining supplies of local building materials like travertine and mortar. At the same time that the papal building agenda was underway, there was an effort to enact a new set of cultural proposals. The *letterati* sought new cultural reforms to rescue the culture of the past, one example being the effort to reconstruct the earliest form of the basilica of Santa Maria Maggiore using early textual sources and recovered objects found under the pavement of the church itself. The Capitoline Museum, which opened in 1735, and then the Corsini Library (1736) exemplified the way architecture embodied culture. Museums and libraries displayed, preserved and organized the past consistent with new ideas on the meaning of Roman culture.

Such building projects started with Augustus, who, more than any of his predecessors, promoted the idea of urban redevelopment. He reorganized Rome into fourteen administrative zones called *regiones*. In addition to focusing on public works, Augustus encouraged wealthy aristocrats to contribute major new buildings to the city, convincing such politicians as Lucius Marcius Philippus and Lucius Cornificius to participate. His own contribution included the temple to Apollo on the Palatine Hill; the Porticus Octaviae and its libraries; a theater dedicated to the memory of the Roman military leader during the Gallic War of 225 BCE, Marcus Claudius Marcellus; and his own forum, with a temple to Mars Ultor. His goal, however, always remained the creation of a monumental city so that arrival in Augustan Rome would be a compelling sight.

On his deathbed, Augustus's last words were, reportedly, "I found Rome a city of bricks and I left it a city of marble." Cities had evolved from their origin as sacred places into civic gathering places that required administrative, cultural, economic and social institutions, while satisfying the demands of a growing and occasionally restless public. Developers often stepped in to bridge governmental and institutional needs, meeting public demands for better and more affordable living conditions. Such placemakers played a critical role in the ancient world and continue that role today. And as Augustus was building Rome to become the largest city in the Western world, a few centuries later on the other side of that world, a Chinese emperor was developing the city of Kaifeng into the largest city in the post-Roman world.

# 06 Land and Loyalty in China

*I have long been fascinated by an unusual work of art, one of the largest and perhaps most renowned paintings in China.* Riverside Scene at the Qingming Festival *was created in the twelfth century to capture daily life in Kaifeng, the central city of the Northern Song Dynasty. The painting is nearly 18 feet (5.5 m) long and contains images of 814 humans, 28 boats, 60 animals, 20 vehicles, 9 sedan chairs and 170 trees. But for me the important thing was the 30 buildings. The countryside and the densely populated city form the two main sections in the picture. But to fully understand the painting there must be a context, a history, which means learning about early land development in China.*

URBAN DEVELOPMENT flourished in China in the tenth century CE (an early example of urban renewal), notably in Kaifeng, in east-central Henan province. In Henan, the rulers, much like Augustus in Rome, promoted private investment to encourage people to settle on unoccupied urban territory and rebuild the city's long-neglected core. Suddenly, development meant something, since the right to buy and sell property as a commodity depended on market prices, which in turn depended on commercial value determined by the parcel's use. And the almost thousand-year practice of trading and conducting commercial activities only in the marketplace shifted: business could now go on in neighborhoods, away from central markets.

Population growth soon caused overcrowding, requiring urban expansion. The then emperor Shizong of Liao had a simple solution: he ordered Zhao Kuangyin, later Emperor Taizu, to gallop south from the Gate of the Vermilion Bird until his horse became exhausted. That point would mark the limit of the city's southern expansion. Such imperial planning quadrupled the size of Kaifeng, surrounded by a new defense wall 17 miles (27 km) long, with twenty-one gates and an average height of almost 40 feet (12 m).

Initiation of the new landholding policies began with the military, or rather the fear of the military: Zhao Kuangyin, soon to be emperor, quickly realized the threat to him posed by his own army, which sought to thwart his drive for increased power. On August 20, 961 CE, he organized a meeting at the capital of the generals who supported him. At a banquet, he persuaded these generals to relinquish their military power, allowing court appointees to serve as governors in the prefectures. Coincident

Emperor Taizu, founder of the Song Dynasty in 960 CE, asked his generals to relinquish military power in exchange for land.

with their altered status, the emperor would furnish them with generous pensions, mansions and substantial tracts of land for their service. Land for loyalty was the way he maintained their allegiance, offering the generals new ways to increase their wealth by encouraging them to develop their land. In Chinese history, this deal became famous as "dissolving military power over a cup of wine."

Emperor Taizu founded the Song Dynasty, which ruled China from 960 to 1279 CE, with the emperor and his successors the principal architects of real estate development in the country. His critical first step, as mentioned, involved the exchange of land for loyalty. To those whose allegiance to him was unquestioned, he granted land parcels, which were passed on through generations. The Song Dynasty was unique in other ways besides its granting of land. It became the first government in the world to issue paper money or banknotes and the first to create a standing navy. The government also encouraged the first use of gunpowder and the discovery of true north with a compass.[1] This same dynasty has been called the start of the "Chinese Renaissance" because of its technological progress and inventions. A new, philosophical interpretation of the old texts led at this time to the revival of Confucianism after the Tang age of Buddhism.

The Song Dynasty also elevated civil scholars over the military: Emperor Taizu restructured his government so that military officials were made subordinate to civilian ones, in contrast to the practice of the preceding Tang Dynasty. Civil officials replaced military governors, accelerating the privatization of land within the framework of governmental law. Over time, however, the movement of land from one owner to another accelerated, and by the time of the Ming Dynasty (1368–1644), a popular saying was that "in one thousand years, a piece of land has eight hundred owners."

1   Y.J. Choi, *East and West: Understanding the Rise of China* (Bloomington, IN: iUniverse, 2010).

But Emperor Taizu went further with his reforms, period-ically redistributing land to males between the ages of eighteen and sixty, using a sliding scale: approximately 1,330 acres (540 ha) went to an imperial prince; 798 acres (320 ha) to serving officials of the upper first grade; 665 acres (270 ha) to those of a lower first grade, and then all the way down the hierarchy so that the director of the warrior cavalry received 89 acres (35 ha). Peasants received 2¾ acres (1 ha) to be held in perpetuity, plus another 10½ acres (4 ha) of personal share land, which reverted to the state upon the death of the owner or when he reached age sixty. The ancient measure of land was the *mou,* which varied with location and region. It was commonly just over 806 square yards, or less than one-fifth of an acre (0.07 ha). The idea of land in perpetuity was to allow for the production of crops requiring a long time investment, such as fruit trees.

But every dynastic Chinese government had to collect from the country's agricultural economy the money needed to fund the imperial house and government, and to maintain the defense of the frontiers, ensure social order, provide relief from famine, sup-port the roads and canals, and uphold control of the trade routes. A proposed twice-a-year tax scheme emerged. With enforcement, monies began to regularly support government programs.

The government disposal of land allowed the government to collect much-needed regular tax revenue. However, a tax exemp-tion meant that privileged landowners paid little or nothing, while the poor paid more. The ruling elite—members of the imperial clan, holders of noble titles and all senior officials—paid noth-ing. The greatest privileges ironically meant the least taxation. The combination of freedom and obligation did not guaran-tee financial allegiance to the emperor, only political support.

The lack of dependable revenue for the government soon became so acute that early in the Song Dynasty the government was forced to collect taxes from officials' estates. Local administrations as early as 962 CE had to compile tax lists for active civil and military officials, and soon an equitable tax system was in place that supplemented the twice-a-year system. Gradually, the landed gentry, who had managed to avoid paying taxes or had paid only minimal taxes, had to meet their obligations.

In contrast to preceding governments and generations, however, once the Song government chose where it wanted walls, buildings and defenses, it allowed all city dwellers, including artisans, traders and merchants, the freedom to purchase land and settle anywhere within a city's limits. This move contained growth and avoided sprawl. Previously, this choice was limited only to the aristocracy or those in much favor with the emperor. Now, financial independence could determine land acquisition and use. No longer was the city defined by its walls or sections; now, there were streets and alleys with shops and residences opening onto streets, while beyond the city gates, commercial suburbs began to form.

Another feature of Emperor Taizu's liberal attitude was the extension in 965 CE of a curfew until 1 a.m., which meant that businesses could operate until that hour—increasing and extending commercial activity. But as interior walls separating districts or wards gradually came down in the city, and businesses now had direct access to the street, commercial land values shifted. For perhaps the first time in Chinese history, commercial buildings became more expensive than private residences. And as the population in Kaifeng prefecture grew from about 890,000 between 976 and 984 CE to about 1.3 million in 1103, the city became the most populous in the world, eclipsing Rome. To accommodate the growth, new buildings were built with even more stories. Towers of restaurants appeared, competing with towered pagodas. Distances between important

The prefecture of Kaifeng, still a bustling metropolis, in 1100 CE exceeded the size of Rome.

# REAL ESTATE
# IN THE NEW CHINA

Beginning in the 1990s, the Chinese government allowed government workers to purchase government-owned apartments — the first step in opening up the country's real estate market. But until the early 2000s, Chinese banks were reluctant to provide loans to average citizens to rent apartments or buy condominiums.

Since 2003, however, cheap credit for the construction and purchase of property has resulted in local governments selling off land to developers for the construction of thousands upon thousands of condominiums, town houses and single-family homes. In just a few decades, with the steep increase in land prices, China's real estate market is now the largest in the world, although the Chinese government still holds control over the land, offering no more than seventy-year leaseholds to buyers.

Real estate development quickly became a driving force in the new economy, with the Chinese government playing a major role in expropriating property to make land available for both public and private large-scale developments. New cities have been forming at the rate of twelve per year. However, dozens of these new cities remain empty, since the owners failed to find tenants willing to move to the new cities or able to pay the rent. The largest among these "ghost towns" is Ordos, a city built for one million people in Inner Mongolia.

As a result of developers building too much too quickly, financial experts fear a real estate bubble about to burst. But that may not necessarily be the case, since China's conservative mortgage lending policies, increased migration to the cities, and rising incomes may soon prove that the high prices are justified and many now empty apartments will soon be occupied. But to counter this glut of not just apartments but whole empty cities, the government has introduced a "one apartment" law, which limits speculators and others to owning only one property.

Nevertheless, the shift to a reformed system of capitalism has resulted in great wealth for a few and the emergence of a Chinese 1 percent class, plus a large-scale class of real estate developers and investors. Ironically, many are investing in foreign real estate, fueling property booms in thirty-five countries around the world. These areas of investment include 27 of the world's 154 largest urban areas outside China, and cities as diverse as Melbourne, Vancouver, São Paulo, and Paris, and as remote as Paphos (Cyprus) and Tamarindo (Costa Rica).

Top: Many of the new developments and new cities in China remain empty. Shown are high-rise apartment buildings in Beijing.

Bottom: Kowloon Walled City, now demolished, was the densest development ever created, an example of what could happen without developers, without architects and without laws.

government offices and institutions also expanded, with buildings, including the Imperial Palace, now within a radius of approximately 25 square miles (64.5 km²).

One important feature of Song land practice was that women not only managed family personal finances but also negotiated the buying and selling of land, supervised the building of houses, kept accounts of rents and taxes, and dealt with other commercial activities outside the family. Such financial knowledge was crucial, since their dowries often included large amounts of land that required administration, which they undertook while their scholar-official husbands were occupied with government business. During this time, another radical idea appeared: widows were entitled to inherit their husbands' property without restrictions.

As the population of cities grew, so too did the need for proper accommodation. The bureaucrats and the laborers required shelter, which intensified the work of developers to maximize space and rooms. As affordable space became scarce, not only property owners but also merchants and the new class of scholar-officials competed to gain the right to develop land. Often with early real estate agents, the officials rented out property, ran guesthouses and started development companies. The court itself was the biggest landlord, as records from the Office for Houses and Shops indicate. Rent was paid on a daily basis to avoid accumulating debts, but this practice often encouraged the government to spend frivolously as its cash on hand accumulated.

The Song Dynasty transformed Chinese society in that it no longer entirely accepted the hereditary power of northern aristocratic families. The new class of scholar-officials trained in Confucian doctrine who were graduates of a competitive civil service exam led a progressive regime. A new society replaced the great families and inherited power of the past. The brother-successor of Emperor Taizu, Emperor Taizong, continued the reforms while expanding his empire, notably defeating kingdoms in Sichuan in the southwest as well as in central and southern China. He also centralized state authority, but to ensure he had loyal civil officials to staff his bureaucracy and provincial administrations as well as ministries, Taizong continued the practice started by his brother, Emperor Taizu: rewarding his men with land. Previous reliance on members of the aristocracy, whose power had come from birth and landholdings, no longer worked. He needed well-educated officials who believed in the new, centralized system.

These reforms consolidated the pragmatism of the emperor, as military leaders worked with knowledgeable Confucian scholar-administrators in fashioning reforms. The key, they realized, was a powerful civilian government. To strengthen civil society, they instituted tax and other monetary reforms. In urban planning terms, these reforms encouraged development and more open designs for cities, which spurred the growth of local markets and national commerce. All this was made possible through Emperor Taizu's distribution of land to the private sector, almost equal in scale to the Great Dissolution of Henry VIII that occurred five hundred years later in England, the topic of the next chapter.

# 07

# Tudor England
# and the Dissolution

Hever Castle, Anne Boleyn's home, was later owned by Henry VIII. In the early 1900s, it was refurbished by businessman John Jacob Astor's grandson with funds received from the sale of the family estate, site of the old Waldorf Astoria hotel, to Al Smith and Jakob Raskob, who built the Empire State Building.

---

*Our friend Gertrude recently turned 107 years old, and my wife, Mary, reads to her twice a week. They read about Tudor and Elizabethan England and have gone through all of Philippa Gregory's steamy novels. Their favorite character and heroine is Anne Boleyn.*

*A few years ago while Mary and I were on the south coast of England, and driving to visit Henry II's newly restored and refurbished Dover Castle, Mary, my astute companion/passenger, spotted a sign on the highway that read HEVER CASTLE TURN LEFT. We turned and soon arrived at Hever Castle. Anne Boleyn's family home turned out to be a château built within the walls of a medieval fort, surrounded by spacious and well-manicured grounds and gardens.*

*It was to Hever Castle that Henry VIII came to woo Anne. They married in 1533. Three years later, when Henry was unable to get a divorce, Anne was accused of various sins on false charges and was beheaded. The property, built in 1207, became Henry VIII's after the death of Anne's father, Thomas Boleyn, in 1539. Henry, in turn, bestowed Hever Castle upon Anne of Cleves in 1540 as part of the settlement following the annulment of their marriage. Hever Castle still has one of Henry's private door locks, which were taken with him on his various visits to noblemen's houses and fitted to every door for his security.*

IN 1536, centuries after Emperor Taizu of the Song Dynasty distributed land to the military, Henry VIII acted in a similar way. When his first wife, Catherine of Aragon, failed to produce a male heir, he sought a divorce from her from the Catholic Church so he could marry Anne Boleyn. The Church hesitated to grant and then denied his request. He responded by separating England from Rome and established the new Church of England. Most importantly, by 1539, he claimed all of the Church's assets, which constituted 60 percent of the properties of England, including monasteries, chapels, houses of worship and landholdings. This was called the Dissolution of the Monasteries, the greatest transfer of land in English history since the Norman Conquest. In the process, numerous monasteries were destroyed or adapted to secular use.

Refusing to compensate the Catholic Church, Henry VIII did not always retain these properties and their chattels for himself, or for that matter for the public good or for the Crown. He often distributed the real estate to members of the gentry and nobility, at first as a reward and then later for a fee. Monastic land was frequently granted to gentlemen pensioners: for example, Caversham Manor and park, in Berkshire, previously owned by the Reading Abbey, was granted to Sir Francis Knollys. Certain monastic buildings were retained for royal use, often as storage depots for the king's possessions. And former monastic property, specifically White Friars, Black Friars and the Charterhouse in London, were used by the Offices of the Tents and Revels in the 1540s for storing equipment, including stage equipment. The Office of the Tents served both military and festive functions, from assembling a military camp to providing cover

Henry VIII expropriated, without compensation, all Catholic Church property in England and redistributed it in what was called the Great Dissolution.

for receptions, banquets, festivals and occasionally the court if it was traveling.

Another, less well-known source of land for the king was from convicted traitors. Through changes to the treason law of 1534, the Crown could seize any and all land held by a traitor. And between 1532 and 1540, 883 people in England and Wales were tried for treason. Three hundred and eight, or 35 percent, were executed. Their lands were taken by the Crown and their goods either sold off or kept by the king, with the most valuable items sent to the Jewel House in the Tower of London.

People who had property claimed by the king included some of high rank. For instance, Thomas Wolsey was an English political figure and cardinal of the Roman Catholic Church. By 1514, he was a powerful eminence who virtually controlled the business of the state while maintaining his powerful influence within the Church. In addition, he was Lord Chancellor, the king's closest chief adviser. This was not unlike Cardinal Richelieu's role one hundred years later in the government of France's King Louis XIII (see chapter 9).

But Wolsey fell out of favor because of his failure to negotiate an annulment of Henry's marriage to Catherine of Aragon. He was ultimately stripped of his government posts, and he retreated to York. When the cardinal fell out of favor with the king in 1529, he had his goods inventoried and presented to the king. They included a number of tapestries, plus seven carpets, eight chairs and 861 ounces of silver plate. His property and goods gave "the single greatest boost to both the quality and quantity of Henry VIII's possessions," states historian Maria Hayward in a 2013 essay.[1]

Ironically, this massive exercise of eminent domain—in this case, the government seizing the properties of the Catholic Church—was not for a public purpose in the true sense of the term.

1 Maria Hayward, "Rich Pickings: Henry VIII's Use of Confiscation and Its Significance for the Development of the Royal Collection," in *Henry VIII and the Court: Art, Politics and Performance*, ed. Thomas Betteridge and Suzannah Lipscomb (Farnham, UK: Ashgate, 2013), 39.

## DRAPERS PART OF GREAT REBUILDING

Following Henry VIII's Great Dissolution came the Great Rebuilding, with the Drapers joining in the process, as the following passage from Lena Cowen Orlin's *Locating Privacy in Tudor London* outlines:

> The London Drapers joined the Great Rebuilding in 1543. They moved to a new Company Hall, trading up to a property dislodged from its longtime owner (the Catholic Church) by the Dissolution of the Monasteries. They were already substantial landowners and as early as 1538 discussed the real estate investment opportunities made available by Henry VIII's seizure and distribution of Church holdings. At a point, anxiety about the new order of things prevailed... However, in 1543 it appeared that would not be the case, and by 1554 Queen Mary and Philip of Spain reconfirmed the lay ownership of former Church properties taken during the Dissolution. With this new assurance and new investment funds from Thomas Howell, a former Warden of the Company, the Drapers went on a buying spree.[2]

As discussed in chapter 2, Roman property law never dealt with the issue of eminent domain, but the concept—the state's power to take private property for public use—grew in importance over the centuries. In France, for example, the government instituted laws of expropriation so it could rebuild Paris, a project Napoleon III considered to be entirely for the public good (see chapter 11).

Major beneficiaries of the Dissolution and the king's largesse were members of the Drapers' Company, an organization of successful businessmen who raised monies for charity. The Drapers raised their funds through real estate investment and development, including leasing properties they acquired or received from the court as a result of the Dissolution and enhancing their value (see sidebar). Today, the Drapers' Company still has a sizable property portfolio in the City of London.

2    Lena Cowen Orlin, *Locating Privacy in Tudor London* (Oxford: Oxford University Press, 2007), 116.

But the Drapers and other new owners in the sixteenth century, anxious to occupy the monastic guesthouses and abbots' lodgings, were also hesitant. They were reluctant to take ownership of the new properties because they felt the Dissolution could be considered illegal; the king himself was unable to provide them with the certainty of clear title, and they feared that the Church might someday seek to reclaim the property.

The Dissolution and its resulting redistribution of land in the 1500s helped generations to form the vast English estates that later played such a part in the establishment of the picturesque villages of the seventeenth century (see chapter 10) and even the utopian company towns of the eighteenth and nineteenth centuries (see chapter 12). Perhaps the most striking example of redeveloped Church property is what became England's largest palace at the time: Hampton Court, located in

Hampton Court was completed in 1525 by Cardinal Wolsey on redeveloped church property he received as part of the Great Dissolution, and later expanded and transformed by Henry VIII.

Richmond upon Thames in Middlesex, some 11¾ miles (18.8 km) southwest of central London. On land and buildings given to him in 1514, Cardinal Wolsey began to construct Hampton Court, one of the most opulent sets of buildings in the country. The land had previously been part of the Order of the Knights Hospitaller of St. John of Jerusalem. Wolsey worked on the project for seven years, rebuilding the existing manor house to form the nucleus of the present palace. Henry VIII stayed in the state apartments as Wolsey's guest immediately after their completion in 1525.

But Wolsey was to enjoy his palace for only a few years. In 1528, knowing that his enemies and the king were engineering his downfall, he passed the palace on to the king as a gift. Two years later Wolsey died, but within six months of gaining ownership, the king began his own rebuilding and expansion. Henry VIII's court consisted of over one thousand people, and even though the king owned more than sixty houses and palaces, few of them were large enough to hold the assembled court. Thus, one of his first projects, to transform Hampton Court into a principal residence, was to build vast kitchens and then apartments. Between 1532 and 1535, Henry added the Great Hall (the last medieval great hall built for the English monarchy) and the Royal Tennis Court.

Henry VIII became England's leading developer, expanding, for example, York House, the London residence of the Archbishop of York. It became Whitehall Palace, joining Westminster with Charing Cross, a site in central London where the Eleanor Cross once stood (a monument commemorating Eleanor, the wife of King Edward I) in what was the hamlet of Charing. When the Royal Apartments at Whitehall were wrecked by fire in the early 1500s, Henry VIII erected Bridewell Palace (whose name derives from an ancient holy well), south of Fleet Street just west of the city.[3] Henry also built St. James's Palace and the now lost Nonsuch Palace in Surrey (see sidebar). The styles of these structures were often confused, however, with Gothic arches supported by classical columns or medieval ceilings decorated by depictions of Roman gods. Nevertheless, his buildings stood as symbols of royalty.

Further "destructive renewal," the result of Henry VIII's actions, included the Duke of Somerset's use of stone from the St. John Clerkenwell Priory and St. Paul's Charnel House to build himself a magnificent Renaissance palace, today's Somerset House, on the Strand in 1547. The Strand Inn and the Church of the Nativity, as well as the houses of the bishops of Chester and Worcester, were destroyed in order to build the new and grand Somerset House. "The losses of the church presented great opportunities for the City Livery Companies," ancient and modern trade associations of the City of London, and "they claimed many fine buildings for themselves from those left redundant," writes the historian David Nash Ford.[4]

At the end of his reign, Henry VIII owned fifty-five properties, more than any other English king to that date. Ironically, it was the Catholic Church that provided the land and often the buildings that established England's largest real estate developer of the early Renaissance, although protection soon offered a new rationale for placemaking and real estate development: the fortress town.

3    David Nash Ford, "Tudor London," *Britannia* (2013), para. 2, http://www.britannia.com/history/londonhistory/tudlon.html.

4    Ibid., para. 5.

## NONSUCH PALACE

The Dissolution of the Monasteries, the availability of new money and the Great Rebuilding that followed launched a national discourse in Tudor England about architectural designs and standards. It also led to the professionalism of domestic building and the emergence of England's first significant architect, Inigo Jones.

One of the great expressions of that new awareness was Nonsuch Palace in Surrey, built by Henry VIII, named "Nonsuch" because there was no other palace of such size or grandeur in the realm. Designed to celebrate the power of the Tudor dynasty, it did not adapt an old building but was built from an entirely new design in a location selected because it was near one of the king's hunting grounds. The grandeur was intended to match Francis I's Château de Chambord. Henry died in 1547 before Nonsuch was completed, and nine years later Queen Mary I sold it. It returned to royal hands in the 1590s. Although at the time Nonsuch was in private hands, Queen Elizabeth I signed the Treaty of Nonsuch between England and the Netherlands in 1585 at the palace. In 1682–83, the Countess of Castlemaine, Charles II's mistress, had it dismantled, selling off the building materials to pay gambling debts.

The eclectic Nonsuch Palace was commenced but never completed by Henry VIII. It was later demolished to pay off the debts of the new owner's mistress. From John Speed's map of Surrey in his early atlas *The Theatre of the Empire of Great Britaine*, engraved 1610.

**08**

# Fortress Towns: A New Model

The distinctive piazza
and street plan of
Grammichele.

*Normally when traveling, I prefer to rent a car and poke
around, free from any rigid schedule. Sicily, however,
presented a challenge. Since I was getting on in years, I felt
more comfortable not driving myself, so Mary and I hired,
for the first time, a car and driver. Sabrina turned out to be
a gift from heaven. She rented the car, drove it, filled it with
gas and, most importantly, found places to park it. She was
our guide and interpreter. She also helped us via email, prior
to our departure, to plan our itinerary and recommended
accommodation to fit our budget. She coached us on local
cuisine and wines. Nero d'Avola, pressed from a unique
Sicilian grape, has remained our wine of choice to this day
and mercifully is carried by our local wine merchants.*

*In Piazza Armerina, an eleventh-century city, we stayed at
La Casa sulla Collina d'Oro, a charming B and B near the
UNESCO World Heritage Site of Villa Romana del Casale,
with its well-preserved Roman mosaics. The innkeepers of
La Casa were both anthropologists and archaeologists, and
their home had an extensive library. Drawn to one book,
Grammichele, I became intrigued by the story of this fortress-
style radial town. The next morning I asked Sabrina if we
could alter our route and visit Grammichele, which was not
part of our itinerary. She was enthusiastic and said this was
not a problem. We arrived in Grammichele in time for lunch.*

The star fort of Palmanova was built by the Venetians in the late 1500s. Deemed to represent the ultimate form of urban planning, it inspired the design of fortress-style radial towns such as Grammichele.

EXCAVATIONS SHOW that in the ninth and eighth centuries BCE, the ancient town of Tel Beer Sheba in the northern Negev desert in Israel had a radial plan (*tel* means "ancient settlement mound"). The advent of artillery, however, led to the need for the radial fortress. By 1370, huge bombards (early cannons) weighing several thousand pounds were the main form of attack. But they were unwieldy, and soon cannons designed to breach walls by hurling more portable cannonballs of cast iron replaced these heavy stone weapons. During the Middle Ages, defensive methods triumphed over offensive ones, but the challenge was to develop a fortress whose walls could be protected from being breached by allowing occupants to fire on any breaching mechanism from any direction. Hence, the radial and multisided fortress plan was developed in the form of a hexagon or octagon with protruding towers.

European fortress towns represented one of the earliest applications of the radial scheme to a modern fortification system. They are also the first realization of complete radial plans in the history of urbanism.

Since its inception around the middle of the fifteenth century, the radial city plan had proved itself a pliant tool in the hands of urban planners: it was economical, effective and reassuring in terms of security for the town's inhabitants. By the 1500s, most planning skills were applied to building fortress towns in radial forms. Indeed, military architects revived the radial plans for cities as military engineering emerged as a specialty separate from that of civilian architecture.

In the late 1500s and early 1600s, during the Eighty Years' War with Spain, the Seventeen Provinces of the United Netherlands built frontier cities, the most famous of which was Coevorden, built in 1597. The building of fortified cities with a radial structure was so important that, in 1600, Leiden University in the Netherlands built a special training center for engineering and land surveying for that purpose.

### Grammichele, Sicily: A Fortress-Style Radial Town

Italy, however, is especially known for its great old radial towns, such as Grammichele, which emerged within weeks from the ashes of a major earthquake late in the 1600s. Juror Dr. Mario Centorbi described the effects of the earthquake of January 11, 1693, which leveled his town of Occhiolà, on the island of Sicily.

> This fierce earthquake lasted for no more than earthquakes take, so that those poor wretches who escaped from those offending stones and fallen rubble, half alive and painful, looking like so many statues, devoid of spirit, could not stand up. Their eyes opened up to the light, and seeing that there was no stone on another stone, the sight dazzled them with tears, and with trembling and fear each one felt his soul going away.[1]

One week after the quake, Centorbi went to the home of Friar de Fera to advise him that Prince Carafa wanted him to start planning a new town. As a reformed friar, de Fera was also trained as an architect.

After an earthquake destroyed Occhiolà, Sicily, in 1693, Prince Carafa built Grammichele in the form of a radial town.

1 Quoted in Giuseppe Pagnano, *Grammichele—Luoghi di Sicilia* [Grammichele—Places of Sicily], trans. Denis Gailor, Edizioni Ariete (Palermo: Kalós Press, [1998]), 28.

In 1602, Tommaso Campanella envisioned a utopian city he called the City of the Sun, which, although never realized, became the model for walled cities and fortress towns.

The prince selected a flat stretch of land that had water and could be easily cultivated. Prince Carafa understood the preeminent importance of location. Within less than two weeks after the catastrophe, Carafa had the site cleared, and artisans and materials were arriving for the construction of provisional housing. So began the planning and building of Grammichele, the town designed to replace the destroyed city of Occhiolà, which at one point had three thousand inhabitants.

Centorbi, Friar de Fera and Prince Carafa laid out the new town of Grammichele around a hexagonal central piazza, inspired by fortress towns as well as by Tommaso Campanella's plan for a utopian community, described in his philosophical work *The City of the Sun,* written early in the seventeenth century (see sidebar).

## *An American Capital with a Radial Plan*

Perhaps the most well-known contemporary radial plan is Washington, D.C., a city laid out by Pierre Charles L'Enfant. Born in Paris, he trained to be an architect. L'Enfant came to America in 1777, serving as an engineer in George Washington's Continental Army and becoming a major. In 1791, President Washington accepted L'Enfant's request to design the new capital city in the District of Columbia. L'Enfant chose a layout similar to the then French capital city of Versailles. He moved ahead with what the U.S. National Park Service describes as

> a Baroque plan that features ceremonial spaces and grand radial avenues, while respecting natural contours of the land. The result was a system of intersecting diagonal avenues superimposed over a grid system. The avenues radiated from the two most significant building sites that were to be occupied by houses for Congress and the President.

## THE CITY OF THE SUN

In 1602, inspired by Plato's *Republic* and his description of Atlantis in the *Timaeus*, the Italian philosopher Tommaso Campanella wrote *The City of the Sun*. Written in Italian, his work was not published until 1614 (in Latin). In it, at a time of conquests, Campanella conceives of a utopian, theocratic society where goods, women and children are "held" in common. He prophesies that this new utopia would be part of a unified, peaceful world, the result of a Divine Plan to be governed by the Spanish kings in alliance with the pope.

But his concept did not stop there. He went on to conceptualize the physical aspects of the city. His vision for the City of the Sun became an inspiration for future utopians, among them Prince Carafa in his development of Grammichele and German theologian Johann Valentin Andreae for his concept outlined in *Christianopolis*, published only five years after Campanella's work (see sidebar page 103).

In *The City of the Sun*, Campanella conceives of a city where seven circles of walls protect and defend its inhabitants, and of the construction of palaces to serve as dwellings for the citizens. The location, on a hillside because of better air, has an ideal climate, encouraging physical health.

Its painted walls are among the most spectacular and imaginative aspects of the City of the Sun. Apart from enclosing and protecting the city, the walls are also the pages of an illustrated encyclopedia of knowledge, depicting images of all the arts and sciences. Walking through the City of the Sun, one would see illustrations of the heavens and the stars, of mathematical figures, of every country on Earth, and of all the marvels and secrets of the mineral, vegetable, animal and human worlds. The internal wall of the sixth circle represents the mechanical arts and their inventors. Knowledge is no longer enclosed in books or kept separate from the people, but available to all.

L'Enfant was exacting: the avenues were to be majestic, lined
with trees and connected visually with "ideal topographical sites
throughout the city, where important structures, monuments,
and fountains were to be erected."[2]

The three commissioners of the City of Washington
appointed by President Washington to oversee the project, having the value of real estate foremost in their minds as well as

2    "The L'Enfant and McMillan
     Plans" (National Park Service,
     U.S. Department of the
     Interior, n.d.), paras. 4 and
     5, http://www.nps.gov/nr/
     travel/wash/lenfant.htm.

understanding the potential for real estate development, wanted to have a printed copy of the plan as soon as possible. This meant they could begin the sale of building lots without delay. L'Enfant irritated them by working slowly and released only sketchy plans. Disappointed by L'Enfant being behind schedule and by his lack of cooperation, Thomas Jefferson wrote a letter (on instruction from President Washington) on February 27, 1792, to L'Enfant dismissing him as city planner.

Some thirty-three years later, in June 1825, L'Enfant died penniless and was buried on a friend's estate in Maryland. But in 1909, his remains were moved to Arlington National Cemetery on a hill overlooking the Capitol. Although L'Enfant did not see it through as architect, the city of Washington survived. L'Enfant's radial plan for the capital endured, although his successor, Andrew Ellicott, made a number of alterations: he realigned Massachusetts Avenue, a major diagonal thoroughfare, and removed five short radial avenues, while adding two additional radial avenues southeast and southwest of the Capitol. He even named the city streets.

Washington's radial plan originated in the European fortress towns built three hundred years before. The influence of the fortress town found expression in the design of other seventeenth- and eighteenth-century cities, among them Ville de Richelieu, built a century before the French Revolution.

# 09

# The Walled City
of Richelieu

*I first went to Montreal in 1960 as the resident architect on Place Ville Marie, a major office and retail complex being developed over Canadian National rail tracks in the middle of the city. The developer was Webb and Knapp, the American developer William Zeckendorf's company. I was working for his architect, I.M. Pei, and specifically for Pei's partner Henry N. Cobb, the project's principal designer.*

*Because I had spent approximately five years in France and spoke a little French, it made sense to the firm that I be sent to Montreal as the resident architect and one of its representatives. My wife and I welcomed the idea, since Montreal represented to us a kind of middle ground between the United States and Europe. I found that French-speaking Quebec has preserved many French practices and institutions that affect real estate development.*

FRENCH CANADA OWES A LOT to Cardinal Richelieu. He advocated for Samuel de Champlain, the governor of New France, and the retention of New France, and oversaw the Treaty of Saint-Germain-en-Laye, which returned Quebec City to French control under Champlain. This permitted the colony to develop into the core of francophone culture in North America. In 1627, Cardinal Richelieu introduced to New France the seigneurial system. Under this scheme, lands along the St. Lawrence River remained the property of the king of France but could be ceded in parcels to, and maintained by, the landlord or seigneur of each parcel under specific conditions. That system remained in place until 1854, when it was considered obsolete and abolished under Lord Elgin, governor general of the Province of Canada; the province lasted from 1841 to 1867, when Confederation created the country of Canada.

But this seigneurial system, instituted by Cardinal Richelieu, assured the solidarity of the French Canadians during the century that followed the cession of the country to England. It is that system, in part, to which the French Canadians owe their national survival during those years. Consequently, Richelieu's foreign real estate development assured both the power of France and the sustained identity of Quebec.

Another legal device unique to Quebec and developed by Richelieu was the concept of *le mur mitoyen,* or "party wall." Legalizing "zero lot line" development, where the property line runs along the middle of a shared party wall, was first institutionalized by Cardinal Richelieu for the development of his town, which he started to build in 1631.

Cardinal Richelieu was the most powerful man in France under Louis XIII during the Thirty Years' War in the 1600s. Richelieu wore red robes and was known as *l'Éminence rouge.*

Armand Jean du Plessis de Richelieu was born in 1585 in Paris into a family of minor nobility. His somewhat prominent father was the seigneur of Richelieu, a soldier and a courier. His mother, Susan de la Porte, was the daughter of a famous jurist. King Henry III granted Richelieu's father the bishopric of Luçon (just north of La Rochelle) for his participation in the French Wars of Religion (1562–98). The family appropriated most of the revenues from the bishopric for private use. The clergy challenged this tax grab by the Richelieu family: they needed the funds for ecclesiastic reasons. It was necessary, therefore, for Armand to enter the clergy to protect the family's source of revenue.

Armand's mother proposed to the king that her son be made bishop, and promoted him toward that end. She was successful, for in 1606 Henry IV nominated Richelieu to become bishop of Luçon, but because young Richelieu was under age, permission from the pope was required. So Armand's mother went to work on the pope. With papal permission secured, Richelieu was consecrated in 1607 and immediately heralded as a reformer.

Built out of stones from a nearby fort he ordered demolished, Cardinal Richelieu's château was grander than Versailles, built by Louis XIV fifty years later. Ironically, the château itself was demolished in the 1800s and the stones used to complete homes in the village of Richelieu.

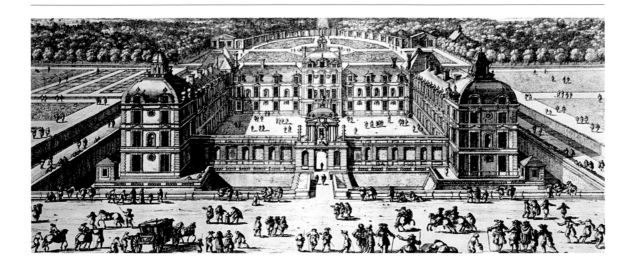

In addition to being a clergyman, he was also known as a noble and a statesman. Two hundred–plus years later, he became a leading character in Alexandre Dumas's *Three Musketeers*. What is less well known about the cardinal is that he was an informed and shrewd real estate developer.

But beginning in 1614, Richelieu went in and out of favor with the king. He was even banished to Avignon for a period before he finally took his place as the king's principal minister in 1624.

Because of his elegance and his red robes, Richelieu was soon labeled *l'Éminence rouge* ("the Red Eminence"). Père Joseph, a Capuchin friar, became Richelieu's confidant and adviser. Not wanting to compete with the cardinal, Père Joseph donned gray robes; as a result, he was soon labeled "the Gray Eminence," hence the term *eminence grise,* used even today for a behind-the-scenes adviser. However, Richelieu was also an autocrat who took authoritarian measures to maintain his power, censoring the press, establishing a network of spies, and preventing the open discussion of political issues in public assemblies. Those who acted against him were prosecuted and often executed.

In his drive to centralize power, Richelieu wanted to restrict the influence of the feudal nobility. In 1626, he ordered all fortified castles to be razed, excepting those at the borders needed to defend the country against invaders. In 1628, in a rather over-enthusiastic interpretation of his own orders, he destroyed the fortress of Loudon to build his palace next to the town. But the cardinal's town of Richelieu, only 10 miles (16 km) to the east of Loudon, and south of Tours, benefited from this demolition, since Richelieu, acting as a developer, used the stones from the fortifications at Loudon to build his town of Richelieu. He saw both financial and political gain from fashioning the new city.

Apart from inheriting the family farm, he bought up most of the remaining land required for the town from his relations and, in 1631, the cardinal embarked on his ambitious project to build his model town and the grand palace next to it.

Richelieu engaged the architect Jacques Lemercier, who had designed the Sorbonne and the Palais-Cardinal (now the Palais-Royal) in Paris. After living only three years in this palace, the cardinal left Paris for his new town of Richelieu. This became a walled town on a grid arrangement. The adjacent palace (equal in size to the Palace of Versailles, built outside Paris fifty years later by Louis xiv), surrounded by an ornamental moat and large imposing walls, was built between 1631 and 1642 and involved nearly two thousand workers.

The town itself is about 420 feet long by 300 feet wide (130 by 90 m). It is accessible by three monumental gates; a fourth, dummy gate exists to respect the symmetry of the whole. Two symmetrically arranged squares organized the plan: Place-Royale (religious) and the Place du Cardinal (now Market Square). The first was the presbytery, also known as the audience, but which is now the town hall, adjacent to a covered open hall and shops. In planning this town, Richelieu and his architect were likely influenced by another cleric, the German theologian Johann Valentin Andreae, who in 1619, less than fifteen years before Richelieu broke ground, described his concept for a new town called Christianopolis (see sidebar page 103). With respect to its form and size, he could have been describing the cardinal's new town of Richelieu.

Of course, buildings alone do not make a town. It needs inhabitants. Richelieu did not want to live alone in his palace next to this new town: to ensure the town's quick settlement, the cardinal imposed no city taxes and offered building lots on an emphyteutic lease basis gratis to his friends and entourage in Paris. (Such a lease normally specifies improvement to the property via construction.) In return, the lessors undertook

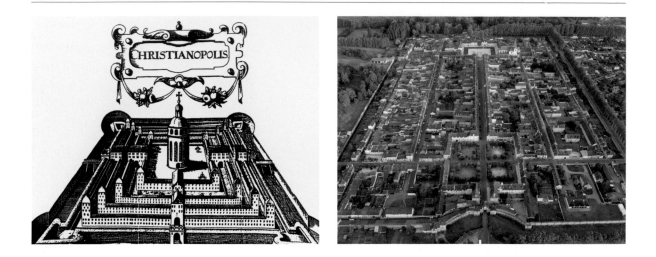

to build a house within two years according to the plans and specifications filed with the court of the city, an early example of design guidelines. These were town houses with *mitoyen* or adjoining walls. The new owners also had to choose a builder who was one of the cardinal's appointees. Importantly, a register of specific transactions was kept, allowing historians today to know who owned the city's original buildings.

All of the cardinal's friends eagerly accepted this offer, for it was not politic to refuse "son Éminence rouge," the most powerful man in France. Friends of the cardinal took ownership of their lots and started to build town houses in accordance with the established guidelines. Incidentally, these same guidelines were used as a model by Baron Haussmann two hundred years later in the reconfiguration of Paris (see chapter 11). Design guidelines

and the *mitoyen* wall are real estate concepts originated by Cardinal Richelieu that are still used today.

In 1642, the cardinal died before his town was
completed. The city then ceased to grow, and many
of the town houses remained unfinished. Notwithstanding this incomplete state, the town continued
to attract renowned visitors, including Voltaire and
Jean de La Fontaine, France's famous writer of fables.
He praised Richelieu as "the most beautiful village
of the universe."

Following the cardinal's death and the decline
of the monarchy, few in France wanted any links
with the name Richelieu. The heirs to the town
houses had no wish to complete them. Even Richelieu's palace became too expensive to maintain and,
after falling into ruin, was eventually dismantled
in the nineteenth century, by a real estate broker
who would sell the stones for scrap. These stones
found unlikely homes in local farmhouses. In the
mid-nineteenth century, well after the French Revolution and during a period of relative affluence,
the heirs of some of those whose homes had been
left unfinished bought the stones from the demolished palace to complete their own town houses
in the town of Richelieu. Ironically, these were the
same stones that came from another demolition,
the demolition ordered by Richelieu of the fortress
at Loudon two hundred years earlier. The town
of Richelieu, although small in scale, exhibited a
remarkable urban environment compared with the
picturesque towns, villages and garden suburbs that
would soon follow in both England and France.

**CHRISTIANOPOLIS**
Designed by Johann Valentin
Andreae, Christianopolis was
a square-shaped town with
700-foot (215 m) sides fortified
with four towers and a wall. It
looked toward the four quarters
of the Earth. Eight other towers
distributed through the city
reinforced and intensified its
strength. In addition, it had
sixteen smaller towers and a
citadel in the middle of the city.
Fresh air and ventilation are
provided for the four hundred
citizens who live with "religious
faith and peace of the highest
order" in the city, writes Andreae
in his 1619 description of the
fortified town of Christianopolis.

# 10

# Picturesque Towns and Garden Suburbs

Bedford Park, on the
western outskirts of London,
was the first garden suburb
in England, a precursor of
the Garden City movement.

*Some years ago, I watched a compelling documentary that dealt with the subject of modern design and asked the question, Why are people willing to accept contemporary design in all aspects of their lives, including appliances, transportation, graphics, commercial buildings, and even apartment buildings, but generally not with respect to their own private home?*

*As part of the answer to this question, the documentary followed an aging English couple who owned a large home on a sizable lot in a traditional residential neighborhood. Their home was too big for them, but they didn't want to leave their neighborhood or the beautiful rear garden. They were advised that their lot was big enough to build a modest second building at the rear of the property. They could occupy this second building through their retirement years while receiving revenue through renting their original home. Because their main objective, in addition to reducing their footprint and simplifying their lives, was to enjoy their garden, their architect designed a simple, contemporary box, with floor-to-ceiling glass facing the garden. After moving into their new "fishbowl" residence, they found the glass wall brought the garden into their home to such a satisfying degree that it was now possible for them to rid themselves of many objects that had previously cluttered their living space. In a short time they adjusted to, and appreciated, their new aesthetic if not ascetic environment. The new is sometimes the best way to adjust to and appreciate the old.*

PSYCHOLOGISTS BELIEVE THAT the attachment to traditional forms of housing, along with our habit of collecting souvenirs, memorabilia, furniture, paintings and other items, promotes a sense of ownership and security. These objects also create a sense of attachment to the past, and—by extension—offer a means to emulate the way aristocracy or at least the well-off lived.

As a result, the romanticized view of the "picturesque house" in the "picturesque village" remains. It came to us through the Dutch and Flemish painters of the seventeenth and eighteenth centuries. The picturesque village, offering visually charming buildings and settings often suitable for a painting reflecting balance and form, has remained a model and ideal for the development of garden cities and suburbs to this very day. One important failed attempt at creating a "picturesque village" was Sir William Ingilby's rebuilding in 1825 of the village of Ripley, next to Ripley Castle in North Yorkshire, England.

Picturesque villages were modeled after the paintings of them by Dutch and Flemish artists, such as *Village near a Pool*, by Meindert Hobbema.

## Ripley Village, Like It or Not

Henry VIII's suppression of the monasteries in 1536 (see chapter 7) caused Yorkshire's established Catholic families to revolt. William Ingilby (1518–1578), the High Sheriff of York-shire, despite being married to a Catholic, received rewards resulting from the Dissolution for his staunch loyalty to the Crown. William and Ann's son, born in 1757, was named John. John married an heiress. His new father-in-law promised him funds to rebuild Ripley Castle, which had belonged to the Ingilby family for over seven hundred years. But Sir John had a disagreement with his father-in-law halfway through the project (losing his construction financing) and went into exile for eleven years, while his estate agents sold timber off the property to pay his debts. By the time he returned to England, his marriage to his wife, Elizabeth, was over, despite her having borne him eleven children. The eldest and heir to the Ingilby estates was John's son William (yet another William), who was a product of a broken home and who became an eccentric.

William, like his father, became interested in building. Although he had no formal training, he studied the craft from a building manual that provided construction details, standard plans and specifications for the application of materials. The manual was published by the Society of Dilettanti, founded in 1734. This society, made up of men of power, was devoted to studying classical art forms, which meant that its members were knowledgeable, appreciated architecture and possessed a general sense of aesthetics. The building manual they published remained in use through the early 1900s.

The nondescript town houses of Ripley, North Yorkshire, were disliked by the locals and inspired a poem deriding the well-intentioned builder, William Ingilby.

William planned to reconstruct the castle in 1827 but in order to house the workers, he demolished the existing village of Ripley, with the aim of rebuilding it as a model estate village. He sought to create a picturesque village. But rather than mimic the standards of a "picturesque village" modeled after the villages seen in French, Dutch and Flemish paintings of the period, or the design standards set out by the Society of Dilettanti, he copied an idea for buildings seen while visiting the Alsace-Lorraine. The result was a community of nondescript town houses, disliked by many locals. One occupant was so disenchanted that he condemned Ingilby in a poem:

Let's be jolly—dance we—tipple we

Old Sir William has left us Rip-e-ly

Blessings on his honoured head

Good alive—but better dead!

The poem popularized the view that real estate developers built only for profit and were "better dead," even if their motives were altruistic. Altruism was certainly the intent of many prosperous English Victorians, who, on land they inherited, often from the Dissolution of Henry VIII, surrounded their great houses with villages. The proposed objective of such estate owners was to improve the conditions of country people and local workers, although these folks could never own their own land.

Building picturesque villages allowed a town to emerge with a certain beauty permitted only because of lax building codes and varied architectural visions. The landowner thus became a real estate developer, initially to add value to his own holdings but also to prove himself a man of taste and goodwill with the satisfaction of carrying out, through the development of his real estate, a philanthropic act.

## The Aesthetic Movement and Bedford Park

By the nineteenth century, with an increased population and a growing middle class needing housing, the suburban speculative developer emerged. The art critic John Ruskin and craftsman William Morris soon revolted against what they saw as mid-Victorian materialism. The vulgarity often generated by manufactured products and industrialization meant for them a need to return to handcrafted works of furniture, decoration and fabrics. Real estate developers who remade many parts of British cities were the focus of a good deal of their criticism. As Morris wrote in *Hopes and Fears for Art* (1882):

> How is money to be gathered? Cut down the pleasant trees among the houses, pull down ancient and venerable buildings for the money that a few square yards of London dirt will fetch; blacken rivers, hide the sun and poison the air with smoke and worse, and it's nobody's business to see to it or mend it: that is all that modern commerce… will do for us herein.[1]

Morris idealistically hoped that there might be an alternative: "Suppose people lived in little communities among gardens & green fields, so that you could be in the country in 5 minutes walk," he wrote in an 1874 letter.[2]

And so the Aesthetic movement and the Arts and Crafts movement began; at the same time, Ebenezer Howard, also in the United Kingdom, introduced a method of urban planning known as the Garden City movement. These three movements were designed to mitigate the dreadful conditions and pollution resulting from the Industrial Revolution. The movements came to North America at about the same time (see sidebar), applying these aesthetic standards mostly to utopian company towns being developed by enlightened industrialists (see also chapter 12).

1   William Morris, "The Lesser Arts," in *Hopes and Fears for Art* (London: Ellis & White, 1882), https://ebooks.adelaide.edu.au/m/morris/william/m87hf/complete.html.

2   William Morris, March 26, 1874, in *Collected Letters of William Morris. Vol. 1, 1848–1880*, ed. Norman Kelvin (Princeton, NJ: Princeton University Press, 1984), 218.

# ARTS AND GARDENS
# IN WESTERN CANADA

The Arts and Crafts and Garden City movements came to Canada in the early 1900s in the design of the town surrounding a new paper mill in Powell River, British Columbia, traditional territory of the Coast Salish people.

The development of the mill was the result of three historical events occurring almost simultaneously. They included the discovery of hydroelectric power, first applied in Niagara Falls in 1879, later to be the basis for King Camp Gillette's "Metropolis" (see sidebar page 141); the 1840 discovery in Germany of how to produce paper from wood pulp; and the 1844 invention of newsprint in Nova Scotia, Canada, followed by an exploding number of daily and weekly newspapers being published around the world.

Having depleted Minnesota of its forests, three entrepreneurs—Dr. Dwight Brooks, his brother Anson Brooks and M.J. Scanlon—found at Powell River all they needed to build a paper mill for the manufacture of newsprint. On the shores of the Salish Sea, they found extensive forests to provide pulp, the ability to generate hydroelectric power, and a deep-water port from which to ship their product. The B.C. government, anxious to encourage development in this part of the province, sold the three men 250,000 acres (101,000 ha) for $1 per acre.

These three visionaries, enlightened industrialists and devotees of the Arts and Crafts and Garden City movements, were also placemakers, determined to create a humane environment around their mill. They would do so by adhering to four basic principles:

- The town would be preplanned by Ebenezer Howard.

- Homes for workers would be built on design guidelines consistent with William Morris's Arts and Crafts movement.

- The town would be surrounded by a green belt and farms, as prescribed by the Garden City movement.

- The town would incorporate a mixture of uses, including industrial (the mill), residential, recreational (parks and gardens) and commercial.

To this day, Powell River, now recognized as a National Historic Site, remains a prime example of Garden City planning and home building in the style of the Arts and Crafts movement.[3]

All were reacting to what they saw as evidence of philistinism in art and design, and they encouraged the appreciation of art in everyday life. Suddenly, the relatively plain Queen Anne houses of the period were redesigned to showcase sculptural shapes and intricate details such as oriel windows and shadowed entrances with new, open interiors. The Aesthetic movement emphasized art in the production of stained glass, furniture, wallpapers and books; the exotic and historical blended, and soon the "cult of the beautiful" developed, with a stress on the pleasure to be derived from beautiful objects.

Yet the middle classes could not locate a suitable environment in which these ideals could be expressed. The enterprising Jonathan Carr, however, responded to their quest. Carr was a textile merchant with a taste for property speculation and a vision for real estate development. Through his family connections he married the daughter of Hamilton Fulton of Bedford House, who lived near the new Turnham Green Station of the District Railway at the then western edge of London, near Chiswick. Carr saw the potential of the area around his father-in-law's house. In 1875, he bought 25 acres (10 ha) of land, around and including his father-in-law's house, and set about developing a scheme for a subdivision he called Bedford Park, with the area's well-established trees defining its rural character.

The first garden suburb in England, Bedford Park had winding streets, creating a leafy residential neighborhood that was imitated not only by the Garden City movement but also by suburban developments around the world. Sir John Betjeman, poet laureate of England from 1972 until 1984, described Bedford Park in 1960 as "the most significant suburb built in the last

3  Susan Clark, "Powell River Townsite: A Craftsman-Era Company Town in the Canadian Wilderness," *American Bungalow* 60 (Winter 2008): 28–39.

century, probably the most significant in the western world."[4] Three major factors influenced Carr in developing this concept:

- The Aesthetic movement of the time promoted by William Morris.

- His own desire to create an "elite artistic community."

- The availability of land with easy access to public transportation.

Designed by Richard Norman Shaw between 1875 and 1881, Bedford Park was unique. Earlier park villages near Regent's Park and later Holly Village in Highgate were other attempts at picturesque suburbs, but Bedford Park set a new goal. It was from the outset planned as a self-contained community, with even its own community buildings.[5]

Jonathan Carr selected the ideal site for Bedford Park, close to the train station and large enough for six hundred homes and all ancillary community buildings. This ordnance survey map dates from circa 1894–96.

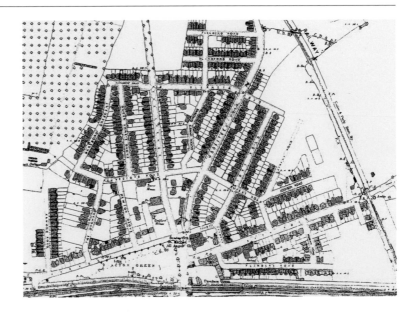

The site Carr selected was ideal with its proximity to the train station where residents could connect to all parts of London within thirty minutes. Carr anticipated a new kind of estate where attractive houses at cheap rents in a semirural setting would appeal. He would retain as many trees as possible. Although his initial idea was to develop Bedford Park simply as an estate with a community of six hundred homes, he soon added a church, inn and shopping area, not to mention a club with a stage for theatricals and debates. Many of the houses also had studios, and early residents included painters, poets, writers, illustrators and general free spirits.

Journalists, playwrights and even ex-military men (attracted to the low rents) broadened the essentially artistic population, which at one time included the playwright Arthur Wing Pinero and the painter Camille Pissarro. The 1881 "Ballad of Bedford Park," whose lines included the following, satirized the artistic population:

> There was village builded
> for all who are aesthete,
> Whose precious souls it fill did,
> with utter joy complete.
>
> For floors were stained and polished,
> and every hearth was tiled,
> And philistines abolished,
> by culture's gracious child.[6]

Even the painter John Butler Yeats and his family rented various homes in Bedford Park over the years, especially important to his eldest son, the youthful poet and critic William Butler Yeats, during the formative period of 1887 to 1889. In Bedford Park, "respectable bohemianism met popular aestheticism," to

4    Quoted in Bryan Appleyard, "Bedford Park: The Enchanted Suburb," *Sunday Times*, April 8, 2013, para. 3, http://bryanappleyard.com/bedford-park-the-enchanted-suburb. Appleyard's novel *Bedford Park* appeared in 2013.

5    For a useful account of Bedford Park, see *A Short History of Bedford Park* (Bedford, UK: Bedford Park Society, 2003) and the Norman Shaw entry on *The Victorian Web*, http://www.victorianweb.org/art/architecture/normanshaw/7.html.

6    Quoted in Peter Murray, "Bedford Park and the Aesthetic Movement," Bedford Park Society, March 28, 2011, http://neighbournet.com/server/common/bedfordparksociety001.htm.

quote the younger Yeats's biographer, Roy Foster. One of the more infamous residents was Serge Stepniak, a Russian anarchist and author of *Underground Russia*, which inspired William Morris.

G.K. Chesterton alluded to Bedford Park often in his fiction of the 1880s, especially its fashionable interest in agnosticism, socialism and occultism, as well as its resolute aestheticism. The Tudor-style homes of wood and stucco, their style repeated throughout the area, achieved a unity with the green streets, maintaining the picturesque style designed by Carr's estate architect Richard Norman Shaw. Morris wallpaper and De Morgan tiles around the fireplaces defined the interiors.

The picturesque village concept reached North America in the mid-1800s in the form of Llewellyn Park, New Jersey, promoted and built by its developers as a retirement community and as "a retreat for a man to exercise his own rights and privileges." [7] The project, commenced in 1853, was soon followed, in 1868, by Riverside, outside Chicago. Developers believed that the precepts of the "picturesque village" would enhance the value of their product and, in turn, the success of their marketing.

By the early 1880s, the heart of Bedford Park was complete, but Carr had already acquired more land and continued to build. The development now started a distinctly different phase but required refinancing via a limited liability company. At the same time, Shaw quit, wearied of Carr's demands and reluctance to pay his bills. In 1886, Jonathan Carr's greater scheme for Bedford Park had an abrupt end: the company created to finance the venture collapsed.

Nevertheless, new developers expanded the estate and construction continued on the remainder of the land, now sold to various other developers. Although many built similar houses, many others did not. This ended Bedford Park's distinctive design in both houses and layout. Without Carr's control, without Shaw

7   R. Wilson, "Idealism and the Origin of the First American Suburb: Llewellyn Park, New Jersey," *American Art* 11, no. 4 (October 1979): 79. Quoted in chap. 9 of *Revisiting Riverside: A Frederick Law Olmstead Community*, "Riverside in the Continuum of Community Design," p. 5, http://www.snre.umich.edu/ecomgt/pubs/riverside/RSchapter9.pdf.

as the principal architect-planner, and in the absence of design guidelines, the community lost its unity in style and purpose.

Bedford Park and the other planned settlements in Europe, originating as far back as the seventeenth century, became development models for later villages and homes throughout Europe, the United States and Canada, and confirmed the idea of private real estate development for profit. Removed from the hands of royalty, the government or the Church, real estate development became in the twentieth century entirely the creation of landowner classes, industrial entrepreneurs and commercial real estate developers.

# 11

# The New Paris of Napoleon III

*During my studies at Pratt Institute, I lived at home in Brooklyn with my parents and shared a room with my younger brother. Anxious to break away, I joined the Reserve Officers' Training Corps and graduated with both a bachelor of architecture degree and a commission in the U.S. Army Corps of Engineers as a second lieutenant. It was one way to leave home gracefully and see the world.*

*During the Korean War, I was given the option of being assigned to Europe or Asia. I opted for Europe, which seemed farther from the action, and was assigned to COMZ (communications zone) headquarters in Orleans, France. After two years in Orleans, during which I met my future wife, Mary, who was working at the time for the U.S. Army as a civilian, I decided to remain in France. We moved to Paris and I took a job with a French-American architectural firm.*

*The years in Orleans gave me the chance to visit the French châteaux along the Loire River, and the move to Paris, where we lived for another two years, gave me a wonderful opportunity to explore that city.*

PARIS, which for years has been the center of culture and fashion, is also the epitome of city planning. Its broad, tree-lined boulevards, culminating in plazas and roundabouts that form focal points throughout Paris, make the city not only grand but also an easy one to navigate. The most important of these boulevards is the Champs-Élysées, whose axis starts at the Rond-Point de la Défense and continues for 6 miles (9.7 km) through Arc de Triomphe, Place de la Concorde and the Jardin des Tuileries to the Louvre.

In 1984, I.M. Pei & Partners (now Pei Cobb Freed & Partners, Architects) were commissioned to resolve the complex problem of expanding the Louvre and adding a new sense of arrival to this world-famous museum. Pei's solution was to expand the museum below ground and to provide a new entrance through a pyramid located in the midst of the Louvre's courtyard on the axis of the Champs-Élysées. At the time this solution was announced, it caused a sensation and great controversy. However, it has since been regarded by the international architectural community, as well as by many Parisians, as the most elegant solution possible given the historic context of the site and resulting architectural constraints. The entire expansion was completed in 1989.

The Avenue des Champs-Élysées, with its cinemas, cafés and luxury specialty shops, is arguably one of the world's most famous streets, and despite the height restriction limiting buildings to six stories, it remains one of the most expensive strips of real estate in the world. In 1616, the queen of France Marie de' Medici decided to extend the axis of the Tuileries Garden with an avenue of trees in what were originally fields and market gardens. The avenue was subsequently transformed by the landscape

The pyramid entrance to the Louvre on the
axis of the Champs-Élysées was controversial
when first proposed by the architect I.M. Pei.

architect André Le Nôtre in 1667 according to the wishes of
Louis xiv. In 1709, the name also would change from the Grand
Cours ("Great Course") to the Champs-Élysées ("Elysian Fields").

The Baroque-influenced architecture of the grandiose
Champs-Élysées is typical of the boulevards designed by Baron
Haussmann, the chief architect of the Second Empire's redesigned
city. As much as Georges-Eugène Haussmann's architecture
influenced what Paris looks like today, this grand street earlier
inspired Haussmann's own plans for Napoleon iii's new Paris
and the extension of the grand boulevard system.

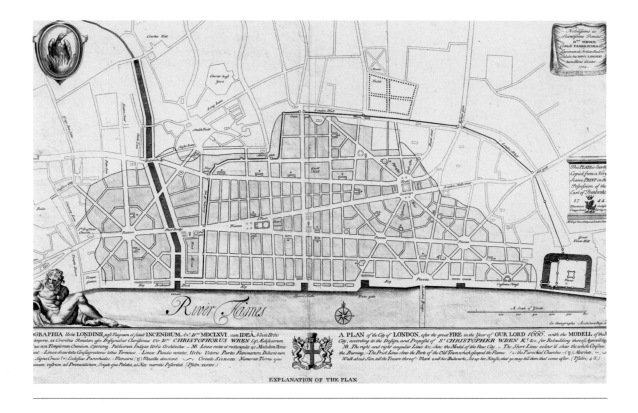

The planning and revitalization of London, shown in a map dating from 1724, inspired Napoleon III to do the same for Paris.

Previously, as Victor Hugo immortalized in the misery of the June Rebellion of 1832, the so-called second revolution, in *Les Misérables*, the city was a warren of dead-end streets and narrow, dangerous roads, easily fortified by rebels. But as the 1848 third rebellion led to the creation of the French Second Republic, with Louis-Napoléon Bonaparte as president, renaming himself Napoleon III, it became clear that the city had to be reshaped for security reasons—and to ensure government control. As ruler of the Second French Empire, Bonaparte held the unusual distinction of being both the first titular "president" and the last monarch of France.

1   "Paris Modernization," *Travel to Europe's Heart* (December 7, 2012), http://traveltoeuropesheart.com/paris-modernization.

Napoleon III had grand plans to modernize Paris, especially after reports of the new urbanization of London inspired by Christopher Wren (see sidebar). Bonaparte had visited London and was impressed. "Our goal," the emperor explained, "is not only to improve and clean up the city but to provide straight avenues and broad boulevards, not easily barricaded, and through which troops might maneuver, so as to better control the capital." He was hardly the first to modernize the city, however. In the midst of the French Revolution, in 1794, a "Commission of Artists" sought to open broader avenues, with a new street making a straight line from Place de la Nation to the Louvre, the location of the current Avenue Victoria.[1]

The idea of a grand plan for a city was not a new idea; ever since the cholera epidemic of the 1830s, which killed twenty thousand, the Count de Rambuteau (prefect of the Seine from 1833 to 1848; a prefect being the chief officer or overseer, from the Latin *praefectus*, "director; one having been put in charge") and the famous physicist Léon Foucault had been calling for new streets so as to "let air in and allow men to circulate." A letter to Baron Haussmann from Napoleon III in 1853 led to major changes. On the recommendation of his good friend and supporter Jean-Gilbert-Victor Fialin, minister of the Interior, the emperor named Haussmann as the prefect of the Seine

## THE REBUILDING OF LONDON

Christopher Wren, known for his architectural contributions to London following the Great Fire of 1666, was by training an astronomer, with a talent for mathematics and invention. One of his inventions was an instrument for writing in the dark. He was a founding member of the Royal Society. His interest in architecture developed from his study of physics and engineering, and his earliest buildings were the Sheldonian Theatre in Oxford and a chapel for Pembroke College, Cambridge. In 1665, he visited Paris, where he was inspired by French and Italian Baroque styles. For the rebuilding of London, where much of the medieval city had been destroyed by fire, he produced an ambitious total plan. However, his plan was rejected when property owners insisted on keeping the sites of their destroyed buildings and developing them independently. Nevertheless, he designed more than fifty new city churches and St. Paul's Cathedral, as well as the Royal Observatory in Greenwich.

district, responsible for making the city healthier, less congested and evocative of grandeur. He held the post until 1870.

Napoleon and his new planner, Haussmann, aimed to liberate Paris from its medieval past of tiny streets, poor sanitation and run-down houses, redesigning it for the modern age. The streets, intersections and architectural scale of Victorian London were a critical influence. At a meeting with Haussmann at the Palais-Royal, the emperor expressed his admiration for the changes taking place in London, which he had recently visited. The city had large parks and an up-to-date sewer system. He wanted such improvements for Paris. Napoleon, Fialin and their financial backers, the Péreire brothers, were also inspired to enact urban improvements by the social utopian philosophy of the Comte de Saint-Simon.

Popular among the educated since the late 1700s, Saint-Simonianism advanced the idea that society could be transformed and poverty reduced by economic improvements spread equally in the society. Saint-Simon was something of a utopian socialist who believed that science and industry would take the moral and temporal power of medieval theocracy and apply it to the contemporary age. He also thought that the government must play an important role in redefining the political and social economy. Aligned with this philosophy, Haussmann would lead the physical, if not moral, modernization of the city as planner and project manager, mobilizing spectacle and public support through parades and demonstrations for the semi-imperial purposes of Napoleon III.

Haussmann wielded an extraordinary level of personal power granted directly from Louis-Napoléon to remake the city, turning its medieval streets, often narrow and stinking corridors with little light and no air, into modern thoroughfares. But this meant cutting wide swaths through the city to establish a system of radial streets and boulevards.

Napoleon III and Baron Haussmann aimed to liberate Paris from its run-down houses, as shown in this 1850s photograph of rue des Marmousets taken by Charles Marville.

Place Saint-Michel became a paradigm of Haussmannism, part of two east-west carriageways connected perpendicularly to the north-south axis Sébastopol–Saint-Michel, one on each bank of the river Seine: the extension of rue de Rivoli and Boulevard Saint-Germain. But the architect and his aides were careful to connect their cuttings with the old roads. The Île de la Cité, however, was a disaster. Haussmann saw it as a warren of crowded shacks and crossed by damp, twisted and dirty streets, perfect for insurrections. He worked to eliminate the labyrinth in what was the historic center of Paris. Haussmann did so by running two large avenues across the island and removing most of the original inhabitants. He similarly implanted the Place de la République on the historical urban fabric of the Faubourg Saint-Antoine area, the Popincourt quarter and the Faubourg du Temple, largely because in this area the "dangerous" working classes lived. Many felt the new vectors of Paris destroyed the character of the city, even if they offered new vistas and visions.

Haussmann's design of Paris streets, including the height of buildings, was highly controlled. New thoroughfares included Avenue de l'Opéra, shown here in a painting by Camille Pissarro.

Haussmann had not only a grand plan but a detailed one, and he closely monitored street furnishings such as gas lamps, kiosks and the design of street urinals, called *vespasiennes*. Alignment was his cause célèbre: he angled the Sully Bridge across the Seine so that it brought the Panthéon into a direct line with the Bastille column, and he moved the Victory column so that it was centered in the newly created Place du Châtelet. He also insisted that the architect Antoine-Nicolas Louis Bailly change the location of the cupola on top of the new Tribunal of Commerce from one side of the building to the other, to create a symmetrical effect with the tower of Conciergerie when viewed from the Boulevard de Sébastopol. Symmetry of the buildings was sacrificed for symmetry of the city.

Military concerns were also a high priority in his redesign. The wide boulevards provided ample space for regiments to march and if necessary keep any rebels penned up in the narrow side streets. Protecting the ability of the state to control the population through the military was crucial. The new spatial relations Haussmann created through his urban transformation of the city had authoritarian as well as cultural overtones. His love of the straight line and uniform construction style dominated his remaking the city.

But as we have seen, Haussmann's grand boulevards would have to pierce existing neighborhoods. To expedite his redevelopment, the French legislature passed several laws under the Napoleonic Code, including one especially for the exercise of eminent

L'Opéra, designed by Charles Garnier,
is one of the first examples of a PPP, or
public-private partnership, development.

domain. This meant the city could acquire buildings in the path
of the proposed new boulevards and streets through expropriation on the grounds that the acquisition was in the public
interest. As a result, the state could legally seize the property of
"holdouts," that is, landowners who blocked the reconstruction
and modernizing of the city.

Consequently, thousands of homes were demolished to permit the "piercing" to make way for Paris's grand boulevards. The creation of the boulevards, as intended, prevented easy barricading. Suddenly, access to public institutions such as the theater or the Louvre became simpler and people congregated with greater ease. Haussmann's boulevards also linked specific nodes throughout the city. For the nodes, he commissioned equally grand projects, one of which was l'Opéra (also known as the Palais Garnier), designed by Charles Garnier (see sidebar page 124).

It took a strong authoritarian regime, like Napoleon III's Second Empire, to encourage capitalists to launch costly but important projects that would benefit both them and the city. The heart of the economic system was the banks, which were at that time undergoing huge expansion. This growth was thanks to their being able to take deposits and the lifting of restrictions on joint-stock banking, which permitted private investors instead of governments to own the banks.

This availability of new capital and Haussmann's grand plans matched Napoleon III's political and economic objectives perfectly. As a result, the redevelopment projects required for the renovation of Paris (like l'Opéra) would be decided by the state, carried out by private entrepreneurs like the Péreire brothers, and financed with loans from the banks backed by the state. The Péreire brothers were prominent nineteenth-century Parisian financiers who were rivals of the Rothschilds. They founded a business conglomerate that included the creation of the Crédit Mobilier bank and held large investments in transportation, utilities, newspapers and real estate.

The redevelopment projects resulted in the total renovation of Paris physically, which resulted in better air circulation. They also led to the better provision of pure drinking water and evacuation of waste. Many of the emperor's critics accused him of hiding under the guise of these improvements and felt that the projects were really geared toward more effective military control of the capital. Yet, the extent of the work shows that Haussmann's and Napoleon's aims were not solely for security or military purposes but included many social and urban benefits, both in the center of Paris and in the surrounding districts: wider streets and boulevards, regulations imposed on building facades, public parks, sewers and waterworks, city facilities, and public monuments were among the projects' accomplishments.

Newly imposed regulations and constraints on the developers, for example, resulted in six-story buildings with what was labeled "the Haussmann facade." Organizing each facade were horizontal lines that continued from one building to another, with balconies and cornices perfectly aligned. The ground floor housed retail shops or cafés; the first floor, offices. The second, third and fourth floors had middle- or upper-middle-income housing, and the fifth floor (under the eaves) had maids' and artists' quarters.

Better ventilated boulevards, with proper sidewalks, encouraged the installation of shops and the establishment of cafés, which in turn encouraged strolling by the bourgeoisie. Despite the strict controls, buildings with multiple uses animated the boulevards and established a new kind of social atmosphere in Paris, where peoples and classes were able to mix. The strolling *flâneur* and café life of the bourgeoisie stimulated leisure and fashion. The newly created boulevard Saint-Germain-des-Prés alone contributed to a culture that has left an enduring mark on Paris's urban history.

But the public at the time deplored the results of the piercing of the neighborhoods, as did Garnier, even though, as architect of l'Opéra, he was the recipient of one the most important

Haussmann's new Paris had a profound impact on the city's cultural life, establishing more cafés, integrating classes of people and helping to launch the city's renowned fashion industry.

public-private partnership commissions in the cultural life of the city. Politicians and writers, including Anatole France and Émile Zola, complained about the spread of speculation and corruption resulting from the rebuilding, and a few even accused Haussmann of personal enrichment. Anatole France went so far as to insult Haussmann one evening at the restaurant Le Procope by loudly announcing to the dining room, "Ladies and gentlemen, let me introduce you to Baron Haussmann, the destroyer of old Paris." On the other hand, there were those who praised Haussmann for creating the "new" Paris. Notwithstanding this praise, soon daily speeches and articles condemned Haussmann and the project of rebuilding Paris.

Baron Georges-Eugène Haussmann was prefect of the Seine under Napoleon III, who gave him a great deal of personal power with which to remake Paris.

The redevelopment of Paris commenced in 1853 and continued for more than two decades. By 1873, toward the end of the project, the government of Napoleon III needed to raise additional funds, which it could no longer do through the public-private partnership process, and so the urban renovations were effectively financed not by loan but by bonds sold through the Caisse des travaux de Paris (Paris works fund), quite outside parliamentary control. After twenty years, Parisians were tired of the constant demolition and rebuilding. The city's finances were also depleted, a situation intensified by its annexing of the resulting suburbs.

In 1870, in order to maintain his waning public support, Napoleon III forced Haussmann to resign. Once he was out of government, Haussmann's fortune dwindled. He retired to Corsica, the French island in the Mediterranean where Napoleon I had been born. Here, Haussmann lived on only the pension of an ordinary bureaucrat, a mere 6,000 francs per year (or approximately $40,000 in 2016 U.S. dollars). To pay all his bills, he had to take on small projects. Not entirely forgotten, in 1877, he was called to the Assemblée nationale to be the Bonapartist party's representative of Corsica. It was a minor position for a great urban visionary and placemaker whose concepts of grand boulevards and squares found new life in the urban redesigns of Brussels, Rome, Vienna, Barcelona and Berlin. In the planning of Paris, Haussmann tried to implement the utopian philosophy of Saint-Simonianism and the world of utopianism. Utopian development soon grew in importance as an attractive alternative to urban density, difficult living conditions and dwindling economic opportunities.

# 12

## Utopias for Profit

On a trip to Los Angeles in 2014, I drove ninety miles north
of the city especially to find the ruins of Llano del Rio, once
a vibrant commune. All that remain are mounds of stones
easily visible from the highway. The rubble came from the
local rio (or river), which fortunately had plenty of stones
but regrettably not very much water. The place is now called
Llano. You could hardly call it a town, for it has only one
building, a post office.

My wife, Mary, and I walked around the ruins of the commune,
which few in the town had ever heard of. It was the month
of March, the air still cool, and mercifully the rattlesnakes
were still hibernating in this desolate site on the edge of the
Mojave Desert. Among the few Joshua trees were the remnants
of one fifty-foot wall of the community hall, some fireplaces
and the cistern. I tried to get a feel for this place and imagine
how it got settled. If it took us an hour and a half to reach
this spot from Los Angeles at 70 miles per hour (110 km/h)
on a paved highway, I could not imagine how Job Harriman
and his thousand followers had got here over rough terrain
in sweltering heat in 1914 to establish this utopian town. Our
visit coincided with the hundredth anniversary of the founding
of Llano del Rio, but there was no celebration. The site is
registered as a California Historical Landmark but with no
markers. Years ago, a few days after a bronze commemorative
plaque was erected, it was stolen; it has never been replaced.

REAL ESTATE DEVELOPMENT and utopias do not at first seem to have anything in common. But both relied on the sale of land for their establishment and the development of industry for their advancement. The ideal town was, of course, a utopia. The notion of a utopia—a perfect, egalitarian and harmonious paradise on Earth—was a recurring theme in literature and storytelling for hundreds of years. It started with Plato's *Republic* (380 BCE) and was repeated in works such as Thomas More's *Utopia* (1516) and Edward Bellamy's *Looking Backward* (1888).

Financial crises, unemployment, poor living conditions, the rise of socialist philosophers such as Karl Marx, not to mention the Reformation, which posited that man could find heaven on Earth and not wait until death to get to paradise—all fueled the utopian dream. The Age of Enlightenment, with its emphasis on reason, followed, something of a backlash to utopian idealism.

Poor living conditions for workers in the new industries advanced the utopian movement in the nineteenth century.

Three types of groups founded utopian communities, in each case headed by a charismatic leader. They can be divided into

COMPANY TOWNS formed by enlightened industrialists (such as George Pullman and his Pullman City, Illinois).

RELIGIOUS COMMUNITIES shaped by spiritualists seeking safe havens for their flocks (such as Joseph Smith's Nauvoo, Illinois).

COLLECTIVES organized by socialists and dreamers (such as Job Harriman's Llano del Rio, California).

The irony of utopian developments was that many were formed not only for idealistic purposes but also for the selling of property. "Utopia" was the hook. Whatever their objectives, most of these communities barely lasted a generation and collapsed for one or more of the following reasons:

THEIR LEADERS were corrupt, were ejected, died or quit, and were not replaced.

YOUNGER GENERATIONS sought freedom and would not be bound by the rules and regulations designed to make the community work and imposed as part of the utopian package.

LACK OF SUFFICIENT REVENUE from local production, from local community and from third-party sources prevented growth.

THEIR HIGH PRINCIPLES FAILED to take into consideration human weaknesses such as jealousy, greed, competitiveness, ego and sexual impropriety.

Practical impediments curtailed the success of utopian communities, ranging from the financial to the political. Contrasting with the ideals of these groups were the realities of everyday life.

## Company Towns in the Age of Industry

Unlike utopian communities, company towns *were* sustainable, supported by the profits from the plant they surrounded, as were those religious communities with a strong economic base. These included company towns such as New Lanark near Glasgow, with its eighteenth-century cotton mills, and nineteenth-century religious communities such as those of the Shakers, with their impressive agricultural and craft industries. Two examples were Oneida, New York, producing silverware, and Amana, Iowa, with its woolen mill.

The Industrial Revolution, a direct result of the Age of Enlightenment, improved productivity through invention and innovations but also required space for machinery, assembly lines and workers. The new large factories required land near their plants to house new bodies of workers. Two types of developers met the workers' housing needs: on the one hand, enlightened owners of industry (many of them Quakers) who believed that better housing yielded better, more dedicated and more efficient workers, and on the other hand, nouveau riche industrialists who had little interest in aesthetic values or social concerns and provided only basic facilities for their employees. In response to the needs of the workers, speculative developers exploited the housing shortage near factories, best described by the American writer Upton Sinclair in his novel *The Jungle*.

In the eighteenth and nineteenth centuries, the utopian ideal was translated into reality as utopian company towns emerged, sites—such as Baccarat (crystal) and Arcs-et-Senans (saltworks) in France; New Lanark in Scotland (cotton); Bournville, a model English town established by the Cadbury chocolate company; and Port Sunlight in England, built by the Lever Brothers for workers in its soap plants. Pullman City, Illinois, was

One of the first utopian company towns surrounds the cotton mill at New Lanark in Scotland, established in 1786 under a partnership that included Robert Owen, a Welsh philanthropist and social reformer.

another example, constructed for the workers at the Pullman train company. What such towns collectively offered employees was an idealized life with few worries: housing, land, education, health care and in some cases even food were all provided.

George Pullman built Pullman City in the 1880s on 4,000 acres (1,600 ha) to supply housing for employees of his eponymous railroad car company, the Pullman Palace Car Company. He wanted a company town next to his factory, partly to address matters of poverty and labor unrest. The town had an artificial lake and a hotel named after Pullman's daughter Florence. He outlined certain standards of behavior workers had to follow, while also charging them rent. Pullman's architect, Solon Spencer Beman, proudly satisfied the workers' needs, his distinctive and comfortable row houses containing such facilities as indoor plumbing, gas and connections to sewers. But Pullman was not a visionary or a philanthropist. He wanted better conditions for his workers because he knew they would be happier and more productive employees.

Pullman City, Illinois, was one of the first utopian towns built in the United States around a factory, offering workers an idealized life with few worries.

The depression that followed the Panic of 1893 reduced demand for Pullman cars. The Pullman company laid off hundreds of workers and switched many more to piecework. This form of employment, while paying more per hour, nevertheless reduced total worker income. Despite these cutbacks, the company did not reduce but rather increased rents for the remaining workers who lived in the town. Workers soon rejected the new conditions, and the town failed as a utopian concept.

### Land Speculation under the Guise of Religion

Utopian towns with a strong religious foundation seemed to succeed when they had a strong economic base. This was the case with the city of Nauvoo in Illinois, developed for the Mormons by their prophet, Joseph Smith, after they were driven out of Zion, Missouri. Nauvoo was called the "Workshop of the Midwest" because of its prolific sawmills, foundries and tool manufacturing facilities. Much effort was spent in these facilities on the construction of covered wagons, which were later used by the Mormons for their trek west and their settling of Utah.

The Vermont-born religious leader Joseph Smith enticed people with the so-called "Promised Land" phrase. With that appeal and the Book of Mormon, he was able to establish the Church of Jesus Christ of Latter Day Saints in 1830, known as the Mormon Church, and, using the Church as a lure, he was able to lead the wanderings of the Mormons from New York to Missouri and then to Illinois, where in each case he sold them land.

Smith may have been a religious leader on the surface, but in reality he was a real estate developer. He played fast and loose in land speculation. As trustee for, and in trust for, the Mormon Church, Smith bought land on credit and sold it for a profit to converts arriving in the city of Nauvoo. Receipts from the land

The prophet Joseph Smith, founder of the Mormon faith, used proceeds from land sales to build the temple shown here, as well as Nauvoo House, to serve as his home and a hotel.

sales were not used to pay back the lenders but, instead, used to construct the Nauvoo Temple, as well as Nauvoo House, which was to be both the prophet's residence and a large hotel he would own and operate.

In his preaching from the pulpit, Smith promoted private land sales in a part of town he owned, ironically called Eden, the residential component of Nauvoo. His high-pressure marketing led to a hasty expansion of Nauvoo. Smith bought yet more land, indebting the Church deeper with creditors, who began demanding payment. Smith held the holy conviction that unlike other American cities, Nauvoo was sacred and did not have to abide by the laws of civil society. At one point he even petitioned the U.S. Congress to recognize Nauvoo as an independent territory. Smith was confident that either the Lord would enable the Church to pay for the land being used to build the "Kingdom" or would wipe out all its debts with a "timely advent." Examining this speculation reveals that the success of the Nauvoo Mormons as builders seems almost as great as their failures in finance.

But a dissident group soon challenged Smith in allocating funds for his Nauvoo House and restricting land sales to his development called Eden. They also accused him of profiteering and published a paper with ads trying to get the Mormon Church to get rid of Joseph Smith and his unprincipled behavior. Smith ordered the destruction of the group's press, which led to his confinement in the county jail. Encouraged by the schism within the Church, anti-Mormon groups from neighboring towns seized the opportunity to halt the growth of Nauvoo. On June 27, 1844, a hostile posse broke into the jail where Joseph Smith and his brother Hyrum were being held for supposedly inciting a riot and shot them. Fearing bloody reprisals, the state government ordered the Mormons to evacuate their "garden city" and leave Illinois. The result was an exodus to Salt Lake City, led by Brigham Young.

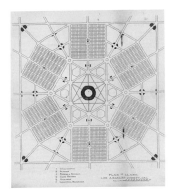

The plan for Llano del Rio mimicked the radial plans of fortress cities and the kind of planning promoted by Campanella's *City of the Sun*.

1    Job Harriman quoted in Dolores Hayden, *Seven American Utopias: The Architecture of Communitarian Socialism, 1790–1975* (Cambridge, MA: MIT Press, 1979), 292.

## A Socialist Experiment in Southern California

The pattern of failure repeated itself, but with a difference, in the story of Job Harriman, a clergyman turned agnostic. After a failed attempt to run for vice-president of the United States, he became the Socialist Labor Party candidate for mayor of Los Angeles in 1910 but lost that election. On the heels of those defeats, he convinced his supporters to establish an alternative socialist town in the Antelope Valley, 90 miles (145 km) north of Los Angeles. Unmindful of the adage "Location, location, location," and of the downfall of the previous communities on the site caused by a shortage of water, Harriman and the town organizers chose this location abutting the Mojave Desert 20 miles (32 km) from the nearest railroad station. They planned to develop this piece of desert "until it was as 'green as the map of Ireland,' but as white [racially] as snow" and founded Llano del Rio in 1914. In promoting his utopian town, Harriman declared, "We will build a city and make homes to show the world… how to live without war, without interest, without money, or rent, or profiteering in any manner, and where the fruits of toil will go to the laborers."[1]

Harriman envisioned Llano as a model multiplied throughout the world. In extending its cooperative ideal, it would become a grandiose scheme of real estate development. But while Harriman and his promoters were advertising "bliss," the residents, who paid $1,000 each and were entitled to a house and a lot, were complaining about the lack of shelter, and then about the poorly built houses when they were finally constructed. These conditions, and the authoritarian style of nonresident decision-makers, might have been better accepted had the site been a healthier one. Its lack of water and poor soil guaranteed its failure.

To design Llano del Rio, Harriman hired Alice Constance Austin (seen at left), a self-taught architect, socialist, feminist and fellow utopian. Austin met with future residents of Llano to explain her design concepts for the new town.

To design Llano del Rio, Harriman hired Alice Constance Austin. A feminist and self-trained architect, Austin shared Harriman's reverence for the family home, and she was also convinced that the political problems of women were reinforced by the designs of traditional dwellings. She was dissatisfied with the role of women in a sexist society and had nothing but contempt for the conventional residences of the day, which confined the feminine personality. In her socialist city, labor-saving devices, central kitchens and laundries would relieve women of thankless and unending drudgery.

Unfortunately, while Austin was busy holding group sessions and developing her plans, the community's financial problems worsened. By the fall of 1917, it was clear that the dream of a socialist town at Llano del Rio would not be realized. Late in 1917, Llano del Rio rallied its most stalwart citizens: they packed up their possessions and boarded a chartered train for Stables, Louisiana, where they took over another unpromising site and named it New Llano.

Harriman was not happy in this new environment. He became ill and returned in 1920 to Los Angeles, where he died in 1925. New Llano, however, had one hope of prosperity beyond subsistence farming: oil, possibly discovered on its property. Regrettably, all test wells proved dry. Although the Depression years provided an influx of new members seeking economic refuge, subsistence living subdued even the most enthusiastic followers and, like other utopian communities, New Llano failed. Idealism transformed into reality meant the demise of the best-intentioned utopian communities.

In post-Renaissance literature, utopianism appeared as a minor theme, again undone by financial or practical causes. By the early twentieth century, it had lost its currency. Utopia means "nowhere" in Greek. Samuel Butler's satirical novel *Erewhon* (1872), which uses an anagram of "nowhere" as its title, indicates the struggle to sustain a utopia. The theme of utopia was soon replaced by its opposite, dystopian literature, showing life imagined as poverty and decay. George Orwell's *Nineteen Eighty-Four* and Aldous Huxley's *Brave New World*—as well as Anthony Burgess's *Clockwork Orange* and Margaret Atwood's *Handmaid's Tale*—emphasize the culmination of utopias in the modern age. Although all utopian communities attempted in the past have failed, the idea lives on. Many utopian communities have been conceived, but many have never been realized, such as Andreae's Christianopolis (see page 103), Campanella's City of the Sun (see page 93) and King Camp Gillette's Metropolis (see sidebar).

## IMAGING METROPOLIS

Wisconsin-born King Camp Gillette made a fortune inventing the safety razor. In the 1890s, while essentially a traveling salesman, he adapted a form of safety razor already on the market by producing a stamped steel (rather than forged) disposable blade. He patented his new safety razor in 1904. The key was the throwaway aspect, introduced to him by William Painter, the inventor of the modern bottle cap. Painter had suggested to Gillette that he invent a product that the purchaser could use, throw away, but need to buy again. Not an immediate success—men still preferred to use the more dangerous open razors, which had to be sharpened before each use—the safety razor, as its blade improved, grew in popularity.

A utopian devotee of Edward Bellamy, Gillette believed that everyone should live in a giant city he imaginatively called "Metropolis." It was to be built over Niagara Falls. Gillette not only designed the city but also conceptualized all the operational systems. He hired Nikola Tesla, who at the time was competing with Thomas Edison, to design a hydroelectric system powered by Niagara Falls, which in turn would provide the heat, light and refrigeration for Metropolis. Tesla, after whom the contemporary electric car is named, was a futurist inventor, an electrical engineer and the inventor of AC (alternating current). Gillette described the entire project in detail in his book *The Human Drift* (1894).

## MODERN UTOPIAS

Although utopianism seemed have died off during World War I, more recently, China has seen the emergence of several utopian communities. These include New Oasis for Life, with 150 members in Yunnan province, a commune that operates without government approval and struggles to survive despite government harassment. In the small town of Lincang, the group seems to maintain utopian goals, focusing on organic farming, earthly spirituality and unorthodox forms of kinship. Furthermore, marriage, money, supervision and punishment are fully barred in any traditional manner. Class-free living is the ideal, with everyone sharing in the agricultural and cultural life. To mark the spirit of the group, members each take on a new name, such as "Beneficial Ground" or "Peaceful Fate." But the government objects and more recently has challenged the group's land contracts, questioning its thirty-year lease from a local school board.

Another contemporary utopian venture is Auroville (City of Dawn), an experimental township in South India. It was founded in 1968 by the charismatic Mirra Alfassa (also known as "The Mother") and designed by the French architect Roger Anger. Alfassa's first public message about the township echoed Alexander the Great's description of Alexandria. She said, "Auroville is meant to be a universal town where men and women of all countries are able to live in peace and progressive harmony, above all creeds, all politics and all nationalities. The purpose of Auroville is to realise human unity."[2] Although designed to accommodate fifty thousand, Auroville has a current population of approximately two thousand, of which over one-third are from India.

2   Quoted at http://www.auroville-international.org/auroville/auroville-a-universal-city.

Apart from religious conviction, communal living was, and remains, one of the driving forces behind the development of utopian communities. The possibility of sharing similar social and political goals was a major draw. But gradually, as utopian communities came to reflect social perfectibility rather than religious purity, the ideal became more elusive. Coupled with inadequate revenue and political friction, utopias failed. But the desire to live in harmony persisted, undermined, perhaps, by founders who were actually developers and whose idealism was always framed by profit and the pragmatic.

# 13

## Le Vésinet, Shaker Heights and the Railroad

*Like most middle-class boys growing up in America or Europe in the 1940s, as a kid I had a train set. We received them at one Christmas or another, often a Lionel train set or its equivalent. My favorite childhood story was* The Little Engine That Could. *In the 1920s, a magazine series entitled* Railroad Stories *was published monthly and sold for 15 cents a copy, and railroad stories continue to be published to this day. Today, our grandsons as well as our granddaughter could be playing with Thomas the Tank Engine. Since the advent of railways, railroads and real estate development have always gone hand in hand, something recognized in the game of Monopoly, where the acquisition of railways plays an important role. From its inception in 1903, Monopoly taught the value of wealth and has today as its subtitle "The Fast-Dealing Property Trading Game," with railroads still central. This game, with its theme of developing properties with houses and hotels and rail lines, may be an incubator of future real estate developers.*

DEVELOPMENT OF THE RAILROAD and organized transportation dates back as far as the fourteenth century. It started with the introduction of wagon ways and turnpikes, advancing with the use of steel rails and the steam locomotive in the 1800s. The Bessemer process for making high-strength steel, patented in 1856, made possible the construction of tall buildings and the production of steel rails for tracks. That steel rail, coupled with faster locomotives powered by James Watt's steam engine, combined to produce the railroads and rail systems of today, though many are now powered by diesel or electric engines. Some are even magnetic, running above the rails and achieving speeds approaching that of air travel.

Railroads impacted real estate development in many ways. First and most obvious was not only the transportation of people but also the movement of freight to and from cities and ports, freight ranging from raw resources to agricultural and manufactured products. Railroads also opened up new territories and made vast areas of land accessible for development. The railroad companies in North America were ceded large tracts of land in exchange for constructing and operating the railways; this opened up these parcels and encouraged the rail companies themselves to become huge land developers.

As rail travel became part of commuter and urban transportation, the lands surrounding rail stations and the end of rail lines were densified through the building of homes, factories and offices close to the new rail hubs. Also, tracks located within cities led to further development. But these tracks were ugly and took up valuable inner-city land. The combination of higher urban land values and advances in construction technologies made viable the over-building of these large, unsightly rail yards in city centers with modern apartment buildings, office towers and hotels.

As recently as 2013, a Chicago magazine headline read, "Researchers say high-speed rail could fuel US real estate economic booms," as if that were something new. It's not. As far back as 1875, the development of Bedford Park on the outskirts of London, England, benefited from its proximity to rail transport (see page 113). Rail transportation began to play an increasingly important role in the development of lands around the world in the nineteenth century. Take, for example, the case of the town of Le Vésinet, France.

## Country Homes for the Bourgeoisie

In 1837, the first commuter line was installed from Le Pecq, some 11 miles (18 km) west of Paris, and on the way stopped at the edge of the forest of Le Vésinet. This forest had been previously identified by Napoleon III as an ideal location for a convalescent hospital for wounded soldiers and public works employees injured in the building of Haussmann's Paris, if linked to Paris by the railroad.

Connecting the forest of Le Vésinet to Paris by rail (at nearby Le Pecq) in 1837 made the forest and the lands around it accessible for development. Developers offered free rail passage to residents for ten years.

The mid-1800s was the golden age of construction in France, following the Napoleonic Wars, when Napoleon III was active in reshaping Paris with his planner, Baron Haussmann (see chapter 11). As the city grew, along with its bourgeois population, demand also grew for a "house in the country" away from the city. Advertisements of the day read, "Every important man in commerce or industry should have a desk in the city but his jewel box, that is his home, in a wooded grove near Paris."[1]

Le Vésinet was just such a "wooded grove," the first *ville-parc* built in France. Suburban development emerged in the early 1800s not only to enhance estates but also to house estate workers and employees of new industries. Such houses on smaller lots were a way, too, for an emerging middle class to emulate the rich without the expense of acquiring and maintaining large estates.[2]

Several stars aligned in 1855 to make the real estate development of Le Vésinet a reality: the existence of the forest, a cooperative government, a railroad link to Paris and the meeting of two men—Alphonse Pallu and Charles de Morny, Duke of Morny—and their identification of a financial opportunity that met the political and social goals of the Second Empire.

The duke was an important member of Napoleon III's entourage and ready to use his privileged political position to launch projects as long he could enjoy a piece of the action and remain in the background. This was his intent when he introduced his successful industrialist friend Pallu to the entrepreneur and banker Henri Place. By 1855, Place had acquired a series of diverse properties around Versailles and Saint-Germain-en-Laye and was hoping to exchange them for a large, consolidated parcel, which he intended to exploit by adding value through additional land assembly and real estate development. After discussions with the Duke of Morny and Pallu, and recognizing that the

1   Auguste Villemot, "La vie parisienne dans croniques de Figaro," *Tome 1* (Paris, 1858), in Sophie Cueille, *Le Vésinet: modèle français d'urbanisme paysager, 1858–1930*, trans. H. Auerbach, Cahiers de l'inventaire 17 (Paris: Imprimerie nationale éditions, 1989), 25.

2   For details on Le Vésinet, see Cueille, *Le Vésinet*, cited in the previous note.

forest of Le Vésinet was prime for development, Place established a development company. He funded the company with the help of several friends and named Pallu its general manager. Operating within a well-oiled environment organized by the duke, the company was able to advance things quickly, and by 1856, Place exchanged lands for 1,077 acres (436 ha), or almost all of the Le Vésinet forest.

The real estate development company undertook to build roads, streets and waterworks, and to sell or lease the resulting lands—a vast development undertaking requiring substantial financing. The Parisian banker Ernest André supplied the necessary financing; he had already been successfully speculating in real estate development during the first half of the nineteenth century and understood the projected market. This was the emerging bourgeoisie who wanted to emulate the aristocratic tradition of having a grand mansion near the capital.

Developments in England were also influencing this practice of placemaking near major cities in France. English ads for suburban real estate developments appealed to people wanting easy access both to nature and the city:

> Those businessmen forced to live in London made certain to have a home in the country, where they could breathe pure air, rich in hydrogen and good for the health. It is here in his country house that he could in the evening be close to his family, and cleanse his lungs of the gases he was obliged to absorb during the day in the city.[3]

With similar ads, Pallu launched the marketing of Le Vésinet. As an added incentive, he managed to convince the rail company to provide residents of Le Vésinet with free passage—a gift that lasted for more than ten years. The development of Le Vésinet would not have been such an extraordinary story in the nineteenth century if not for the railroad and the fact that Pallu was a successful businessman and also an ethical one. He was an aesthete with exceptional taste who surrounded himself with an extremely talented development team. Pallu's forceful personality made certain that Le Vésinet would be built in his image and become an ideal community for its inhabitants. Part of assuring this "ideal" was that all buildings in Le Vésinet, not unlike those in Richelieu, had to conform to a set of design guidelines established by the development company and its landscape architect, the Count of Choulet.

Today, Le Vésinet remains the most prestigious suburb outside Paris. In its day, Le Vésinet was considered the third wonder surrounding Paris, after Versailles and the Bois de Boulogne, representative of the new school of landscape architecture emerging in Europe and North America. Its vast parks, riverlets, lakes and tree-lined streets executed by Choulet were inspired

Today, Le Vésinet, with its elegant homes built to strict design guidelines, remains the most prestigious suburb outside Paris.

3   Roger Rouvières, "Histoire et description pittoresque de Maisons-Lafitte," quoted in Cueille, *Le Vésinet*, 26.

by the picturesque villages of England. These English villages also inspired Frederick Law Olmsted, America's first landscape architect. Olmsted designed Central Park in New York City and Mount Royal Park in Montreal. He also designed America's first planned suburban community, Riverside, completed in 1869 on 1,600 acres (650 ha) of land outside Chicago.

### Ohio's First Garden Suburb

On the other side of the Atlantic in the U.S., the railroad played an equally important role in the development of Shaker Heights, Ohio, incorporated as a village in 1912. Shaker Heights got its name from a local religious group, the neighborhood planned on land formerly owned by a group called the Shakers, who were actually the North Union Colony of the United Society of Believers in Christ's Second Appearing.

Architectural writers and city planners have called Shaker Heights "the most spectacular" of early American suburbs, partly because it sits on a plateau east of Cleveland that rises sharply above the city. In 1961, when Shaker Heights was celebrating its fiftieth anniversary, a tenth grader, in an award-winning essay, called Shaker Heights "the ideal community." None of these comments would have surprised Oris P. or Mantis J. Van Sweringen, the bachelor brothers whose development efforts resulted in this highly praised American town.

From the time Oris Paxton and Mantis James, two years younger, ran errands, sold newspapers and lit streetlamps in Cleveland during the 1890s, they impressed their employers with their ability to carry figures in their heads. After five years of working for others, they took their first step into real estate by acquiring a twenty-four-hour option to buy a piece of land that they immediately flipped, making a $100 profit. The quick turnover and profit convinced the two brothers, at the ages of

Shaker Heights was built on land originally owned by the religious group the Shakers, known for their simple and sterile buildings.

twenty-one and nineteen, to embark on the business of real estate. They were close-mouthed, private businessmen who during the ensuing years created an intricate business empire.

In 1905, the Van Sweringen brothers bought the Shaker Heights site, envisioning the first garden-styled suburb in Ohio. In addition to building homes, the brothers set aside land for churches and schools, and they planted trees. The suburb's first name was Shaker Village, but it was soon renamed Shaker Heights. It is known for having rigorous building codes and zoning laws that have helped to sustain the values of the community. Almost 70 percent of the city of Shaker Heights is listed in the National Register of Historic Places.

When the Van Sweringens failed to convince the New York, Chicago and St. Louis Railroad (nicknamed the "Nickel Plate Road") to extend its rail line to Shaker Heights, they acquired the railroad and established their own interurban streetcar system that would carry residents of Shaker Heights to and from downtown Cleveland. Above the terminus in Cleveland, they built a large office complex. Residents of Cleveland call the system the Shaker Rapid Transit.

## Building over the Tracks

In North America, over-building of rail lines and railroad stations started with the construction of Grand Central Station in New York City and its terminal tower. Electrification of the engines made it possible in 1913 to build a new terminal covering more than sixty-seven tracks on two levels. One of those tracks was a secret connector to the newly amalgamated Waldorf Astoria hotel, used by General John J. Pershing in 1928 and later by President Franklin Delano Roosevelt. Covering the tracks in turn freed up prime real estate for development along Park Avenue, and the railroad sold above-track air rights for apartment and office buildings.

Top: The Van Sweringen brothers bought the Shaker Heights site (and the local railway), their first real estate venture, which they envisioned as the first garden-style suburb in Ohio.

Bottom: Homes in Shaker Heights, as in the towns of Richelieu and Le Vésinet, were built in accordance with strict design guidelines.

In 1903, the New York Central Railroad built a six-story
railroad station appropriately name Grand Central Terminal
at Forty-second Street and Park Avenue. Colloquially, the
terminal at the base of the tower was known as Grand Central Station. It originally had a giant blackboard for arrival
and departure information, later replaced by a flip panel
board, the sound of its ever-changing information panels a
fascination for travelers. Another feature was the decorated
ceiling in the main concourse, an astronomical vision of the sky.

The station's forty-four platforms cover 48 acres (19 ha). The station itself was designed to support a tower above it and, in 1954, the New York real estate developer William Zeckendorf proposed a replacement: an eighty-story glass office tower to substitute for the terminal building. A year later, a new proposal replaced Zeckendorf's: a tower of lesser height and mass for north of the terminal, to replace an existing six-story office building. Proposed by Erwin S. Wolfson, the fifty-nine-story building was accepted after modifications. The Pan Am Building, as it was called—now the MetLife Building—was completed in 1963. At the time it was considered the largest office building in the world in terms of square footage, but its gigantic size, dwarfing all the buildings in its vicinity, made it unpopular.

Construction of the Pan Am Building bought some much-needed time for the declining New York Central Railroad. Facing bankruptcy in 1968, it merged with the Pennsylvania Railroad to form the Penn Central Railroad. But the Pennsylvania Railroad faced its own decline and in 1964 demolished the ornate Pennsylvania Station (despite pleas to preserve it) to make way for a more profitable office building, the new Madison Square Garden and the future development of the Hudson Yards.

Needing cash, Penn Central Railroad unveiled plans in 1968 for yet another tower over the tracks. This one was to be designed by the internationally acclaimed Bauhaus architect Marcel Breuer and would be even larger than the Pan Am Building. The proposed structure would use the existing structure at the base, which was designed to support a tower. However, the project would preserve the station's main facade and its world-renowned main concourse. But there was huge opposition from New Yorkers to the plans and to the owners of the Pan Am Building. Most important was the response of Jacqueline Kennedy Onassis:

> Is it not cruel to let our city die by degrees, stripped of all her proud monuments, until there will be nothing left of all her history and beauty to inspire our children? If they are not inspired by the past of our city, where will they find the strength to fight for her future? Americans care about their past, but for short term gain they ignore it and tear down everything that matters.[4]

The Pan Am Building (1963), although retaining the famous Grand Central Station, was a jarring juxtaposition with the neoclassical style of the station.

4 Jacqueline Kennedy Onassis in Charles River Editors, *Grand Central Station: The History of New York City's Famous Railroad Terminal*, Kindle edition (2015), http://www.amazon.ca/ Grand-Central-Station-Railroad-Terminal-ebook/dp/ B00TG2UKGM.

The New York City Landmarks Preservation Commission deemed Grand Central Station a landmark six months before Breuer's plans were unveiled, and the railroad was unable to secure permission from the commission to proceed. The company sued and the ensuing case, *Penn Central Transportation Co. v. New York City* (1978), became the first in which the U.S. Supreme Court ruled on a matter of historic preservation. The court's decision saved the terminal because according to New York City's Landmarks Preservation Act, the action did not constitute a "taking" of Penn Central's property. The action was deemed a reasonable use, in legalese, of government land-use regulatory power.

Across the border to the north, the government-owned Canadian National Railway or CN Rail amassed large landholdings required for its tracks, which fanned out and covered three major blocks in downtown Montreal. Recognizing the value of these

air rights, the rail company had a master development plan prepared for the three blocks in 1923. Because of the Depression and subsequently the advent of World War II, the plan was never realized. After the war, however, the mid-block was developed with a new central station, office building and the luxury Queen Elizabeth Hotel—all three, buildings without distinction. The prime rooms of the hotel facing the city and Mount Royal Park to the north also overlooked an ugly hole in the ground full of railroad tracks that not only served cross-country travelers but also were used as commuter lines from the town of Mount Royal. This community, not unlike Shaker Heights, had been developed by the railroad on lands it owned north of Mount Royal, Montreal's landmark mountain.

To develop the site over its railroad tracks, CN Rail invited the American developer William Zeckendorf to Montreal. Zeckendorf, a great placemaker, held a reputation for high-quality city building. He had perfected his skills in real estate finance and development, through assembling land for the United Nations Headquarters in New York City and his highly successful and groundbreaking Mile High Center in Denver.

And thus was built Place Ville Marie, designed by I.M. Pei's partner Henry N. Cobb. When completed, it was the largest and tallest building in the Commonwealth.

But exceeding the railroads in importance for placemaking, and marking the true advance of real estate development, was the high-rise, literally the next big thing.

## A RAILWAY AS PLACEMAKER

*"A mari usque ad mare"* (From sea to sea) was the original motto for Canada, which came into use only after British Columbia joined Confederation in July 1871 and the Dominion extended from the Atlantic to the Pacific.

Sir John A. Macdonald, prime minister at the time, promised British Columbia a rail link to the east if it entered Confederation. In 1881, legislation confirming an agreement with a syndicate of five Montreal men was given royal assent. The Canadian Pacific Railway (CPR) was incorporated the next day, and work on the railroad began. As inducements to build the railroad, the agreement provided cash incentives and tax relief for twenty years. In addition, the new company was ceded 25 million acres (10.1 million ha) of land along the rails' right-of-way.

The railroad, in turn, made the land accessible for development and enhanced its value many times over. CPR rapidly became the largest developer in Canada and used some of these lands for its famous line of glamorous hotels in cities near its stations. Among these were the Château Laurier in Ottawa, the Château Frontenac in Quebec City

and the Hotel Vancouver in Vancouver. The company also developed resort hotels designed to attract tourists riding the new rail line or traveling on Canadian Pacific steamships. These hotels included the Château Montebello near Papineauville, Quebec; Château Lake Louise in Alberta; and the Empress Hotel in Victoria, British Columbia.

In addition to hotels, CPR developed residential communities on the lands it received, including but not limited to Shaughnessy Heights in Vancouver, named after the railway's first president. Like CN Rail's Town of Mount Royal development outside Montreal, Shaughnessy was designed following the guidelines established by Ebenezer Howard's Garden City movement and marketed as an exclusive community.

Marathon Realty, set up in 1963, was responsible for developing, selling and/or leasing what was left of the 25 million acres (10.1 million ha) for residential, industrial and commercial projects. But as the need for rail yards in the inner city diminished, Marathon disposed of or developed those properties, as well as air rights over the remaining tracks.

# 14

# The High-Rise and the Empire State

*Mary and I were married in Paris in 1958. Following the legalities at Neuilly's hôtel de ville, the wedding party went to Maxim's of Paris for an elegant celebratory lunch. We were greeted by François Vaudable. He had been directing the restaurant with his father for years, contributing to the glory of the enterprise.*

*The next time I met Vaudable was two years after our wedding lunch. In 1960, he came to Montreal at the invitation of William Zeckendorf, who, much to the delight of Jean Drapeau, the newly elected mayor, wanted Vaudable to operate the proposed "Maxim's de Montréal" at the top of his soon-to-be-completed tower at Place Ville Marie. As the project's newly appointed resident architect, I stood on the deck of the freshly poured concrete at 737 feet (225 m) above sea level. Along with Zeckendorf and Vaudable, I admired the view and listened to Zeckendorf wax on about how great it would be for Maxim's to create a restaurant here.*

*Vaudable acknowledged that it was a stunning location for a restaurant. "But where will zee kitchen be?" he asked. Because of the limited amount of space that could be built as an afterthought on the top of the building, the kitchen, said Zeckendorf, would be located in the basement forty-five floors below and service the restaurant via a dedicated high-speed elevator. "C'est ne pas possible," Vaudable exclaimed. He threw up his hands and declared, "If zee kitchen is more zan 25 meters from zee farzest table, you cannot have zee great restaurant and you cannot serve zee haute not to mention zee hot cuisine." And that ended that.*

DEVELOPERS, like termites, forever try to build "higher," and they have been doing this as far back as the construction of the Pharos in Alexandria and the development of apartment buildings in ancient Rome. Until about the mid-1800s, the use of iron, wood or masonry for the structure, and the need to climb stairs, and in many cases the city's building code, limited buildings to six stories. Even though the Eiffel Tower, built in the late 1800s of iron, is equivalent to an eighty-story building, and certain churches, monuments and pyramids exceeded six stories in height, their forms were not suitable for office or apartment buildings. The six-story limit, established by Augustus in Rome, applied to all of Haussmann's Paris and remained the standard until the invention of steel and the elevator.

Although steel was being made in India as early as 300 BCE, it was the invention of the Bessemer process in 1856 that ushered in a new era of mass-produced lightweight steel. Steel soon replaced iron and made the construction of high-rise structures possible. But building more than six stories was still not practical until Elisha Otis improved the elevator, although contrary to popular belief, he did not invent it. The elevator was invented in 1850 by a New Yorker, Henry Waterman. In 1852, Otis invented the braking device that made using elevators for buildings higher than six stories possible and safe.

With the advent of steel and the elevator, the true race to go higher began in the early 1900s in Chicago and New York City, where the term "skyscraper" was born. Some analysts feel that in man's (not woman's) case, the quest for height is phallic in nature and driven by a male desire to conquer. Others say the urge is driven by pure economics (e.g., the World Trade Center) or

Al Smith and Jakob Raskob, developers of the Empire State Building, instructed their architect, "Make it as high as you can without it falling down." When completed in 1931 after fifteen months of construction, the building was the tallest in the world.

simply the need for identity or for marketing purposes (e.g., the Chrysler Building) or, in certain locations, the wish to capture the "view" (e.g., Burj Khalifa). However, in the case of Manhattan's Empire State Building, height was the result of sheer hubris.

When it was completed in 1931, the Empire State Building became the tallest building in the world, reaching to 102 stories. It retained that honor for forty years, until the ill-fated Twin Towers of the World Trade Center opened in 1973. The Empire State Building, named for the state in which it was built (New York State's nickname is the "Empire State") was constructed in just fifteen months, a marvel of construction technology and logistics at the time. Its construction was made possible by the ability to produce and assemble high-grade structural steel, not to mention the availability of skilled steelworkers, many of whom drove to work every Sunday night from the Mohawk reserve outside Montreal and returned each Friday evening to be with their families.

A prevailing myth says the Mohawk made good high-rise steelworkers because these First Nations men were not afraid of heights. This is not true; they were as afraid of heights as anyone. Rather, they made good steelworkers for two reasons. First, for some, their only recreation as kids was climbing the structure of the Honoré Mercier Bridge, after it was completed in 1934 over the St. Lawrence River next to their reserve. So they did have a level of comfort with climbing. Second, Aboriginal people were not able to get work easily in Montreal.

In the National Film Board of Canada's documentary *High Steel*, directed by Don Owen, the narrator, a Mohawk from the Kahnawake reserve working in Manhattan, tells the history of his people working on the Quebec Bridge construction of 1907. "That's a job we Indians never forget," he says. "For Indians, it was a first big chance to prove themselves as ironworkers." But on August 29, 1907, in the early afternoon, the Quebec Bridge collapsed under its own weight due to faulty calculations. Seventy-five workers were killed, thirty-three of them Mohawk—almost the entire wage-earning population of Kahnawake at the time.

As higher buildings of steel were going up in New York City, the Mohawk were sought out as "ironworkers," and the work paid well. The good pay, however, was still lower than what was received by white workers, because the Mohawk were not permitted to join unions. But being a steelworker developed a sense of pride among the men, and becoming one was a tradition handed down from father to son. One of the famed workers was nicknamed "Spudwrench," after the long-handled wrench that ironworkers used to tighten bolts.

Although the Empire State Building came in under budget because of lower wages for the Mohawk and lower building-supply prices during the Depression, it was still not economically viable as a commercial venture and was a failure as rental office space. Even former New York governor Al Smith's smooth tongue and Irish blarney could not do the job of leasing the building to much-needed tenants. The Depression made leasing the space difficult, and for a while it was called the "Empty State Building."

What, then, sustained the developers, kept them economically alive and able to pay off the construction financing? The building's height and its resulting views. Locals and tourists came in droves and paid dearly to ride the high-speed elevators to the 108th floor to admire Manhattan from the building's observation deck. The deck (an afterthought) became a major profit center for the developers and remains one today for the building's current owners.

Job Harriman, founder of Llano del Rio, was not the only failed politician to become a real estate developer. Those behind the Empire State Building were an unlikely and inexperienced pair: Al Smith, ex-governor of New York State and failed candidate for the presidency, along with his financier buddy J. Jakob Raskob. The Empire State Building was their very first real estate venture.

Al Smith inaugurating the Empire State Building. The building was Smith's first real estate venture, undertaken after his failed bid to become the first Catholic president of the United States.

During the 1928 presidential election, Smith ran against the Republican candidate Herbert Hoover, whose campaign slogan was "A chicken in every pot and a car in every garage." Ironically, it was Raskob's concept for financing the purchase of cars "over time" that made the "car in every garage" portion of Hoover's campaign a reality. As a result of a close relationship with the wealthy du Pont family (they had invested in chemicals), Raskob advised the family to buy a controlling interest in General Motors in 1925. They did and appointed Raskob chief financial officer of GM. Through his scheme for financing auto purchases "over time," Raskob changed the automobile industry, increasing sales and enhancing the profitability of GM, while making the du Ponts richer.

Despite this success, Raskob sold his shares in GM and left the company because of a dispute with the chairman, Alfred P. Sloan, to become national chairman of the Democratic Party, a position he sought in order to support his good friend Al Smith's bid to be elected the first Catholic president of the United States. But Smith's crushing defeat left the presidential hopeful without a job, and both he and Raskob were demoralized and in need of something to do. They sought a project and not just any project. They wanted one that would keep them busy and earn them money but, more importantly, one that would restore their dignity and self-esteem.

By this time, Raskob had soured on the stock market and was looking at what was happening to the booming real estate market in New York City. He was impressed and decided to enter the game. He did so in no small way, bringing Smith along as his development manager and a person who, he felt, could turn on his Irish charm and use it to lease out empty floors of office space. Without any prior experience, the two jumped into the real estate business in a most daring and risky way.

The Chrysler Building (1931),
constructed as a symbol of the
car manufacturer, held the title
of "Tallest Building in the World,"
but for only eleven months.
The Empire State Building held
that title for forty years.

In the late 1920s, Raskob's old GM rival Walter P. Chrysler
was building the Chrysler Building, not on speculation but as
an identity symbol and headquarters for his company. Raskob
was determined to build a building higher than Chrysler's and,
in fact, build the tallest building in the world. He recognized
that such a tower would bring renown not only to the building
itself but also to the owners, the city, himself and Smith—not to
mention satisfy his desire to better Chrysler. So his instruction
to the structure's architect, William Lamb, was "Make it as high
as you can without it falling down."

With Pierre S. du Pont putting up the seed money and the
funds needed to acquire the land at Fifth Avenue and Thirty-fourth

Since its completion in 2010 and as of this writing, Burj Khalifa is the tallest building in the world and the tallest man-made structure of any kind, at 2,716½ feet (828 m).

Street in New York City (the original site of the Astor home and later the site of the Waldorf and Astoria Hotels, two separate establishments), the project proceeded and ended up being built to 102 stories. This was higher than the original 85-story project and surpassed by a couple of hundred feet the Chrysler Building, which at the time was the tallest building in the world. The Chrysler Building kept that title for only eleven months.

For good measure, and anticipating transatlantic zeppelin travel, Smith and Raskob added a 200-foot (60 m) mooring tower to the top of the building. How passengers in an airship tethered to a tower more than a hundred floors above the street would descend hundreds of feet to the uppermost floors of the Empire State Building was never resolved. In fact, only one airship was ever tethered to the tower, and in that case for only a few minutes.

Even though it lost its place as the "world's tallest" building after forty years, the Empire State Building remains iconic. It continues to draw thousands of tourists daily, including in 2014 Prince William and his wife, Kate, the Duke and Duchess of Cambridge. It has been the object of many battles over its ownership. Despite the investment economics not originally making sense, it is still sought after as a prize merely for the prestige of being the building's owner. As a result, it was traded from time to time as a trophy building. At one time, a Japanese tycoon acquired it as a gift for his daughter; Donald Trump made an unsuccessful play in 2000 to acquire the building. When real estate tycoon Harry Helmsley bought the high-rise in 1961, he did so not for its poor economic return but rather for the lucrative property management contract that went with it.

Today, ambitious new buildings in the United Arab Emirates, China and Japan dwarf structures such as the Empire State Building and the former World Trade Center. For example, Burj Khalifa (see sidebar) was designed to be the centerpiece of a large-scale, mixed-use development that would include thirty thousand homes, nine hotels on 7.4 acres (3 ha) of parkland, plus nineteen residential towers, the Dubai Mall and the 30-acre (12 ha) artificial Burj Khalifa Lake.

And there are again plans for Frank Lloyd Wright's Mile-High Illinois building: considered a dream in the 1950s, the one-mile-high proposed skyscraper is periodically revisited as a possible project. But would it be feasible technically? Engineers and architects have faced the technological challenge, although financing may be the biggest hurdle. However, if built, it would be the tallest building in the world, four times as high as the Empire State Building and almost twice as high as Burj Khalifa. High-rises mark the most visible forms of placemaking but also the most expensive. Developers cannot resist them, and public demand for urban living spaces, preferably with a view, increases. The intermingling of the two desires suggests future high-rises of even greater magnitude.

Engineers and architects are rising to the challenge. Although the development of graphite building materials and ways to design vertical transportation systems and methods for distributing services may render mile-high buildings feasible, financing, psychological aspects and security challenges may prove to be greater obstacles than technical difficulties.

## HIGH-RISE CITY

As the largest city in the United Arab Emirates, Dubai is home to 911 completed high-rises. More than 88 of them stand taller than 590 feet (180 m). Burj Khalifa, completed in January 2010, rising 2,716 ½ feet (828 m) and containing 163 floors, is, not surprisingly, the tallest building in the city. The tower is also the tallest building in the world and the tallest artificial structure of any kind. The Princess Tower is the second-tallest building in Dubai, at 1,358 feet (414 m), but the world's tallest residential skyscraper. The skyscrapers of Dubai are, for the most part, crowded around three locations, the first along Sheikh Zayed Road, the longest road in the UAE, with seven to eight lanes in each direction. The next spurt of towers developed at Dubai Marina, the marina city actually an artificial canal built along a stretch of the Persian Gulf. When completed, the approximately ten high-rise buildings will form what will be known as the "Tallest Block in the World," led by the Pentominium, which is expected to be 1,693 feet (516 m) and have 122 floors.

# 15

## Suburbs, Shopping Malls, Automobiles

*One benefit of studying architecture at Pratt Institute in Brooklyn
was that all of our teachers were practicing architects. As a result,
most of us were able to secure jobs after school and during the
summer in their architectural offices. I had a job with the office of
I.M. Pei, at that time a division of William Zeckendorf's real estate
firm Webb and Knapp. While at I.M. Pei's office after graduation
in 1954, and while the office was working on a design of the
Hyperboloid for Zeckendorf for Grand Central Station, I was part
of the design team working on plans for the new Roosevelt Field
shopping center on Long Island.*

*As an airfield, Roosevelt Field served as the takeoff site for famous
aviators such as Amelia Earhart and Wiley Post. Charles Lindbergh's
solo transatlantic flight took off from Roosevelt Field in 1927.
After the airfield was closed in 1951, Zeckendorf bought the site for
redevelopment. Although Zeckendorf included retail components
in many of his urban projects, his prior attempt to build a stand-
alone shopping center as part of a mixed-use development in
Hartford, Connecticut, had failed—blocked by the Auerbach family
(no relation) who owned Fox's, Hartford's major department store.*

*But Roosevelt Field would succeed. The $35-million project opened
in 1955 as a single-level open-air mall. In his biography, Zeckendorf
claims it was the largest mall in the United States at the time.
Over the years, it has been added to and enclosed, and the last
expansion, in 2012, rendered it the second-largest shopping mall
in New York State.*

AFTER WORLD WAR II, America's military-industrial complex had to be put to peacetime uses. At the same time, the war production economy had generated much wealth ready for investment. With the return of thousands of war veterans eager to marry and start families, and just as eager to move away from the crowded cities, the suburbs seemed like an attractive idea and a new opportunity. William "Bill" Levitt, a builder and real estate developer, recognized and grasped this opportunity.

Born in 1907 to a Jewish immigrant family, Levitt became president of the development company founded by his father, Abraham. Before World War II, they built and sold upscale homes on Long Island. During the 1930s, they built the North Strathmore community at Manhasset, New York, on the former Onderdonk farm and property owned by the Vanderbilts.

After a decade of providing gracious settings for lawn parties and social gatherings, events the Levitts would never have been invited to, Abraham Levitt bought a 100-acre (40 ha) property owned by the Vanderbilts. He developed the Strathmore Vanderbilt community, centered on an existing French-style château at the end of the long and winding tree-lined drive. Those living in Strathmore Vanderbilt received deeded membership shares to the Strathmore Vanderbilt Country Club.

During the war, Bill Levitt was a lieutenant in the U.S. Navy Seabees, which was similar to the army's Corps of Engineers and responsible for military construction. Following the war, and upon returning to the family business, he realized that veterans and others wanting to escape the city needed affordable housing. Because of their previous and extensive development activity in the area, Levitt & Sons knew Long Island well. It chose for its

Bill Levitt returned after World War II to take over his father's development company. He recognized the need for affordable housing to serve returning veterans who wanted to start families and escape the city.

new development an area known as Island Trees in Jerusalem (Hempstead Plains). Island Trees was named for an ancient grove of pine trees; and Jerusalem, for a Quaker settlement started in 1640. The area had been bought up by immigrant German potato farmers, but when they were hit with an outbreak of a pest called the golden nematode in the 1940s, many of the farmers were happy to sell off their fields to the Levitts. The company named its new site Levittown.

Levitt's innovation in creating this planned community was to have enough volume so the houses could be constructed as if they were on an assembly line. Unlike earlier attempts at mass-produced housing in factory-based assembly lines, where the workers remained fixed and the product moved down the line, in Levitt's home building, the assembly line was reversed. In Levittown, the product (houses) obviously could not move, but the work crews did.

Levitt's other innovations, in addition to assembly-line technology, were avoiding unions, union regulations and union wages by making each laborer an individual subcontractor and paying him not by the hour but by component, similar to the way pieceworkers are paid in the garment industry. Hence, a mason might be given $25 for each brick chimney he built. The mason as a subcontractor brought in his family to help. Efficiency was high, there were no delays on the site and productivity soared, the incentive being that the more chimneys the mason built in a day, the more money he made.

Houses were completed at the rate of several per day, and residents started moving into Levittown in 1947. Levitt himself financed the houses, which sold for between $6,995 and $8,000. But if Levitt could not build houses the way Detroit built cars, he could certainly sell them the same way. Applying Jakob Raskob's marketing technique for selling cars "over time," the Levitts accepted monthly payments as low as $57, a bargain even by 1947 standards. "Levittowners" became the nickname of the new residents.

Levitt & Sons ultimately built more than 140,000 houses and turned a cottage industry into a major manufacturing process. Nicknamed the "King of Suburbia" and credited as the father of the modern American suburb, Bill Levitt rapidly symbolized the new suburban growth with his mass-production techniques to construct in large numbers homes selling for under $10,000. Although he did not invent the building of communities of affordable single-family homes within driving (or commuting) distance of major employment areas, his modernizations popularized this type of affordable housing and planned community in the years after World War II.

Other developers across the country soon created their own Levittowns. Suburban housing and planned communities

## EXPERIMENT IN PREFABRICATED HOUSING

Impressed with the mass-produced, prefabricated housing in Europe, the U.S. Department of Housing and Urban Development (HUD) began in 1969 to explore prefabrication through a project entitled Operation Breakthrough. In the early 1970s, I was president of Descon/Concordia, a company that submitted a proposal to HUD, and we became the only foreign company to secure a contract to build prefabricated concrete multistory housing in three U.S. cities. I had the opportunity to meet HUD secretary George Romney (formerly CEO of American Motors Corporation). He asked me, "Why can't we build houses like we produce cars—one every twenty minutes?"

"We can," I told him, "but we can't put a house on a lot every twenty minutes." Continuing, I said, "Detroit wouldn't be building cars either if it had to build the roads cars ride on." The scale of production, difficulties in land assembly, local jurisdictions and laws, as well as union constraints, were making the prefabrication of most types of housing difficult if not impossible in the United States and Canada.

grew to unprecedented numbers in the United States. These were hardly the picturesque villages envisioned by the Dutch and Flemish painters, however. As a backlash to the conformity of postwar suburbs, decades later, the return of the picturesque village in modern form occurred through the design movement called New Urbanism, which promoted walkable neighborhoods containing a range of housing types. It found its initial realization in Seaside, Florida, a new town built in 1980 by Robert Davis on 80 acres (30 ha) of land he inherited from his grandfather. The master planned community, designed by Duany Plater-Zyberk & Company (credited with being the creators of New Urbanism), emulated comfortable, small-town Southern enclaves, emphasizing pastel houses and picket fences. "The common sense of a community" was its goal.

In 1980, a new form of suburbia emerged in the form of neo-traditional planning or New Urbanism, as applied to the design of Seaside, Florida, by architects Duany Plater-Zyberk & Company, which established strict design guidelines that included fences.

### The Automobile and Shopping Arcades

But the development of suburbia and the shopping centers that served them would not have been possible without the advent of the automobile. By 1922, there were 7.2 million cars on the streets of the United States alone, and many of them could be found in Kansas City, where the first shopping center catering to cars would soon be built.

After World War II, Americans were beginning to travel. Many returning veterans, who had experienced the European and Asian marketplaces, preferred a type of shopping where one interacts with a series of individual shopkeepers in one location. This was the tradition of Trajan's Market in ancient Rome, with its 150 shops on two levels, or the Grand Bazaar of Istanbul, built in the fifteenth century. Tehran and Damascus also had covered shopping areas with concentrated commerce. One of the first purpose-built mall-type shopping areas was Gostiny Dvor in St. Petersburg, which opened in 1785. More than one hundred

Left: In 110 CE, Trajan's Market in Rome—one of the earliest known shopping malls—housed 150 shops on two levels, without any anchor tenants.

Right: The Victorian-era Cleveland Arcade was one of the first indoor pedestrian-oriented shopping arcades in the United States, an architectural showplace.

shops filled the area. Arcades and enclosed shopping centers soon emerged in France, England and Germany.

In the United States, the shopping arcade began in 1828 when the Westminster Arcade or Providence Arcade (locally known as "the Arcade") was built. This historic building in Providence, Rhode Island, was the first enclosed shopping mall in the United States. Developed and designed by architects Russell Warren and James Bucklin in the style of a Greek temple, it had an arcade complete with Ionic columns at either end. Greek Revival was the preferred architectural style of the New Republic, which likened its democratic state to that of Athens.

The Cleveland Arcade, a cross between a lighted court and a commercial shopping street, was among the first inner-city pedestrian-oriented indoor shopping arcades in the United States and an architectural success. Two sides of the arcade had sixteen hundred panes of glass set in cast-iron framing when the building opened in 1890, representing a prime example of Victorian architecture. It was modeled after the Galleria Vittorio Emanuele II, located in Milan. The Cleveland Arcade is a unique architectural triumph of nineteenth-century urban America and one of the few remaining arcades of its type in the United States. Designed by John Eisenmann, it was financed by John D. Rockefeller and several wealthy Clevelanders of the day.

### Shopping Centers on the European Model

The suburban shopping mall, with the automobile dictating its location and often its size, took shape as an air-conditioned, enclosed space that would soon include professional offices and, perhaps, a medical tower. The availability of cheap land on the outskirts of town united with more and more automobile ownership, coupled with sympathetic zoning laws, made the assemblage and acquisition of large tracts of land needed for stores and parking possible. Not only did the suburban shopping mall change the shopping experience, in many cases, it also destroyed main streets throughout North America. Such threats and changes created a new, niche market of consultants who advised small towns on how to fight mall and big-box developers and save their main streets.

Shopping centers in North America have evolved through many stages, from the uncovered, open-air or strip mall to the enclosed mall and the megamall, to festival shopping followed by big-box retailing. Strip malls were built, as were commercial parking lots, to generate revenue that would cover carrying

The size and location of
suburban shopping malls
after the 1920s, such as
Southdale Center in Edina,
Minnesota (pictured), was
dictated in part by the
automobile. Southdale
Center, which opened in
1956 in Edina, southwest of
Minneapolis, was the first
indoor multi-level mall in
the United States, designed
by Victor Gruen to be a
gathering place.

costs and taxes in order to "hold" or "bank" the property until it became more valuable through inflation, creeping development or, ultimately, the ability to rezone it for higher density and/or higher and better uses.

Southdale Center was the first indoor, multilevel shopping center in the United States. It was developed in the mid-1950s by the Dayton Corporation, owners of Dayton's department store in Minneapolis and predecessor of the Target Corporation. In this case, the real estate developer was a department store, whose owners recognized that they could lever their presence and sell space around their store by creating a shopping mall.

To design Southdale, Dayton hired Victor Gruen, an Austrian immigrant who had just completed the design of Northland, an open-air mall outside Detroit. Gruen sought to design not just a suburban shopping complex but a communal center, where socializing at cafés was as important as shopping. He was inspired, no doubt, by places like the Café Museum (1899) and the American Bar (1908), both in Vienna and designed by Adolf Loos, a leading architect of Austria's Secession movement.

Gruen modeled Southdale after the arcades of European cities and in particular after Italy's enclosed pedestrian shopping mall, Galleria Vittorio Emanuele ɪɪ in Milan. Gruen placed the shopping center at the center of a 463-acre (187 ha) development to be made up of apartment buildings, houses, schools, a medical center, a park and a lake. Southdale was to be more complete than urban Minneapolis but not a suburban alternative to downtown. And it was to be better planned. Gruen wanted to create an environment of excitement, leisure and intimacy, accomplished by placing decorative lighting, art, fountains, tropical plants and flowers throughout the mall.

Southdale Center became a magnet for the greater Twin Cities of Minneapolis and St. Paul, Minnesota. Variety was achieved

Architects for the Cleveland Arcade and later the Southdale Center modeled their shopping centers after the Galleria Vittorio Emanuele ɪɪ in Milan, a famous enclosed pedestrian mall.

by the inclusion of conveniences and such facilities as a grocery store, post office and pharmacy. The official mall opening on October 8, 1956, drew forty thousand visitors to the three-story, 800,000-square-foot (74,000 m²) facility. Today, the mall boasts 1.3 million square feet (121,000 m²).

Although the mall itself was a success, Gruen did not achieve his vision for development around the shopping center. But he was a visionary, after all, because as department stores started to fail in the late 1990s, new merchandising devices were needed to fill these spaces and maintain the draw for the CRUS (commercial retail units). The answer came as development began to encroach on what were once remote suburban shopping centers. Their land value increased to the point where it made sense to replace open-air parking with covered parking, while densifying the site around the mall, which was exactly the kind of development envisioned by Victor Gruen four decades before.

The model of using the department store as the draw or "loss leader" for a mall was a very old formula. It had been used by the circus, where the big top was the attraction but the real money was made on the midway. Modern cinemas duplicate the formula: the movie being screened attracts the audience, but the real money is made at the concession stand.

This was the formula used by all mall developers, and it was expressed in the so-called dumbbell design, claimed by William Zeckendorf to be applied first in his Roosevelt Field shopping mall. This design required two large department stores at either end of the mall, with the plan appearing to look like a dumbbell. The developer would build and lease these large spaces at each end of the mall to department stores (loss leaders) for little or no money just to be able to lease the commercial retail units built along the mall between the larger stores. The

Victor Gruen was born in Austria and launched his career with the design of Northland mall, outside Detroit. He remained a European-style socialist, with little use for America's suburban lifestyle.

rent would be high for small shopkeepers, who were anxious to capture the traffic moving between the two anchor stores (the midway).

Zeckendorf convinced Gimbels and Macy's to bookend his Roosevelt Field project. Soon, shopping centers expanded to include four and even six major department stores or "anchors," thus multiplying the number of malls needed to link the department stores. This in turn increased the number of CRUS to be leased, creating the megamalls of today. As development increasingly encroaches on the suburbs and remote shopping centers, one might properly fear that land will run out. If and when that happens, imaginative developers and placemakers will (and are) turning to space, the next frontier.

## TEXAS MEGAMALLS

Raymond Nasher, from Dallas, was another megamall builder and placemaker. In the early 1960s, to the dismay of many of his developer friends, he leased a 97-acre (39 ha) cotton field on the outskirts of the city on which he built a major shopping mall, NorthPark Center. It opened in 1965 as the largest climate-controlled retail establishment in the world. NorthPark expanded in 2006, more than doubling its size. At over 2 million square feet (186,000 m²), it is the second-largest mall in Texas, with some 230 shops. The Galleria in Houston, at 2.4 million square feet (223,000 m²), is the largest mall in the state. Importantly, from the start, Nasher had his shopping center designed to house his art collection, before he created the Nasher Sculpture Center in Dallas.

Like many real estate developers, Nasher was a serious art collector. He left his sculpture collection to the City of Dallas, along with enough funds to build and maintain the downtown Nasher Sculpture Center.

# 16

# Space and the Future

After the completion of Place Ville Marie in Montreal in 1964, I was offered a position in New York to head up a joint venture to be formed by three major architectural firms, including I.M. Pei & Associates. These firms had been selected to design a multi-use complex, including a new convention center over the tracks of Pennsylvania Station in New York.

As my wife, Mary, and I sat in our garden in Montreal, trying to imagine what life would be like trying to raise three small children in New York City, I determined that it would probably be impossible to duplicate the lifestyle we enjoyed in Canada. Accordingly, I stayed in Montreal and formed my own consulting company. It was a wise move. The New York project did not materialize until decades later, in a different form and with other players. Meanwhile, I transformed myself from architectural consultant to real estate development consultant and soon became the vice-president of development for Concordia Estates Development Company. The company took its name from Montreal's motto, "Concordia salus" (*Salvation through harmony*).

During the continued assembling of land for another project, Concordia Estates responded to a call for proposals from the Canadian National Railway to over-build the third block of its over-the-tracks master plan, south of Montreal's Central Station and one block south of Place Ville Marie. Concordia won the development rights and a 99-year emphyteutic lease (the lessee must improve the property through construction) by proposing

*a vast, 3-million-square-foot (278,700 m²) multi-use concept to include retail, an exhibition hall, a merchandise mart, a world trade center and a hotel. The entire complex was to be called Place Bonaventure (named for the old railway station that had once occupied the site).*

*Architects in Co-Partnership (ARCOP), I.M. Pei's local associate architects for Place Ville Marie, designed Place Bonaventure as a massive Brutalist-style building, fortress-like and for the most part windowless, with roughly hewn concrete exterior walls. When Place Bonaventure was completed, in time for Expo 67, it was the second-largest commercial building in the world. It was a vast project because Concordia's strategy for securing the development rights was to bid the highest amount for the lease of the air rights, which could only be justified by proposing to build a large amount of square footage. CN Rail, on the other hand,* was just as anxious to realize as much money for the air rights as it could.

Except for the 365-room rooftop hotel, the project was a financial disaster for reasons too numerous to mention here. The hotel, however, remained a success. Its low scale (only three levels above the roof), featuring rooms with city views or facing into the lushly planted courtyards, its year-round outdoor pool and its fine restaurants all contributed to make the Hotel Bonaventure an oasis in the middle of the city. Indeed, once in a while, in the middle of winter, we would take our children to the hotel. They loved rubbing themselves in snow and then jumping into the hot pool, and when it was snowing, would surface to stick out their tongues and taste the snowflakes. The hotel with its unique pool not only was popular with visiting businesspeople and tourists but also was often used as a spa or weekend retreat by Montrealers like ourselves. Since we had no TV at home, on July 20, 1969, we rented a suite and the whole family sat on the edge of the king-sized bed watching in awe as Buzz Aldrin and Neil Armstrong landed on the Moon.

## SHOOTING FOR THE STARS

The four partners who owned Concordia Estates were idealistic capitalists with socialist roots. Two of the partners had even been members of the Communist Party of Canada and were banned from crossing the border into the United States. When I joined them in 1960, the company was in the process of assembling six city blocks east of Montreal's McGill University to build what they believed would be the ideal urban living environment—a city within a city. This "utopian" mixed-use project of apartments, retail shops, hotels and offices was to be called Cité Concordia, later redubbed La Cité. To conceptualize the design, Concordia engaged the famed Finnish architect Alvar Aalto.

The project was a massive undertaking that would require the closing and rerouting of streets, as well as the razing of six city blocks of historic greystone houses, rented to McGill students. There was opposition on many fronts, and it took years to secure the entitlements. In the end, the project was only partially realized, regrettably without the guidance of Aalto, who was replaced early in the design process by a smaller local firm. So much for idealism.

Orbital Technologies and Bigelow Aerospace are two futuristic companies working on plans for space hotels.

**WHEN JULES VERNE** published *From the Earth to the Moon* in 1865 and the concept for a space elevator was first published in 1895 by Konstantin Tsiolkovsky, people thought they were mad to be seriously contemplating travel to the Moon and the planets. This was science fiction that would never be realized—space travel was just a fanciful dream. Of course, since then, travel to outer space has been accomplished not only via Moon landings and the International Space Station, but also in probes to Mars and beyond.

All this activity has not gone unnoticed by real estate developers and entrepreneurs. Richard Branson, developer and owner of the Virgin Group empire, which operates Virgin Airlines, has launched Virgin Galactic, which will provide suborbital spaceflights to space tourists. And, if there are going to be space tourists, they will need space hotels, won't they? Not to worry; Russia's Orbital Technologies is on top of that opportunity, planning to launch a space hotel in 2016. Stays in the space hotel (officially named Commercial Space Station) will range from a minimum of three days to a maximum of six months. Among other challenges, supplying the hotel with fresh sheets and towels might present a genuine logistical problem.

Thinking even bigger, Las Vegas–based Bigelow Aerospace, another space hotel entrepreneur that sells inflatable bubble habitats for infinity and beyond, is filing for an amendment to the 1967 Outer Space Treaty to allow private individuals to own sections of the Moon. "No one anything [no one country] should own the Moon, but yes, multiple entities, groups, individuals, they should have the opportunity to own the Moon," company founder Robert Bigelow told CNBC.

The Outer Space Treaty, created by the U.K., U.S. and Soviet governments in 1967 and administered by the United Nations, is the basis of today's space law and has 102 signatories. Article 2 states: "Outer space, including the Moon and other celestial bodies, is not subject to national appropriation by claim of sovereignty, by means of use or occupation, or by any other means."[1]

Notwithstanding this treaty, the so-called Lunar Republic Society is selling "real estate" on the Moon, and you can buy 1 acre (0.4 ha) of the Sea of Tranquility for $37.50. If you buy 10 acres (just over 4 ha), you can save up to 40 percent, with further discounts when the society holds a Cyber Moonday sale. Not a bad price for "waterfront" property. Of course, properties are less expensive along the Sea of Vapors. The society's ad states, "Nothing could be greater than to own your own crater!" It goes on to assure you that "your purchase will be registered in the Lunar Registry and you will receive an elegantly printed, personalized parchment deed, certificate of ownership with full mineral rights." This almost seems like satire taken from Jonathan Swift. In *Gulliver's Travels*, Swift has Gulliver survive on the flying island of Laputa, a world devoted to mathematics and the arts.

To buy lunar property, you have to belong to the Luna Society, which is the largest organization promoting private ownership of the Moon. Its development arm Lunar DevCorp proposes to build homes and hotels on the Moon.

### Lunar Embassy Pitches Property for $27 per Acre

In true American fashion and in the spirit of free enterprise, the Luna Society has competition from the California company Lunar Embassy, which claims to be "leaders in the extraterrestrial real estate market and the ONLY company in the world to… possess a legal basis for selling and registering extraterrestrial properties!" In 1980, Dennis Hope, the founder and owner of the Lunar Embassy, filed a declaration of ownership of the Moon in a San Francisco country office. He also declared himself omnipotent ruler of the lunar surface, giving himself the exalted title of "The Head Cheese."

1    United Nations Office for Outer Space Affairs, *United Nations Treaties and Principles on Outer Space, Related General Assembly Resolutions and Other Documents* (n.d.), Article 2, p. 4, http://www. unoosa.org/pdf/misc/SpaceLaw/ STSPACE-61Rev1_-_English.pdf.

More than 300,000 people, including three former U.S. presidents, have bought real estate on the Moon from the Lunar Embassy alone. The company is selling lunar land at $27 per acre, and the company is making a fortune. It also sells property on other planets. Dennis Hope is telling customers he has the right to sell off the Moon under a loophole in the UN's 1967 Outer Space Treaty. Although the treaty forbids governments from claiming the Moon, it is silent as to private ownership, leaving Dennis Hope, as he has done, free to claim it. But Martin Juergens, a German businessmen, says the Moon belongs to him, because Frederick the Great claimed the Moon in the eighteenth century and gave it to the Juergens family. "Juergens has no paperwork," says Hope.

You do not have to limit yourself to the Earth's moon, where there may be territorial conflicts and court battles with the heirs of Martin Juergens. In 2010, the Lunar Embassy announced, ironically, the largest land sale in the history of the Earth—it is offering for sale property throughout the solar system in the form of entire satellites of Mars, Neptune, Saturn and Uranus.

Not to be outdone by American entrepreneurship, these two companies have recently been joined by the U.K. firm Moonestates, whose inventory of property is limited to the Moon, Mars and Venus. All these companies tout the purchasers' ability to make profit by reselling their property. So far I have not found a resale market on either eBay or Craigslist, nor to my knowledge is it possible as yet to purchase lunar property with bitcoins.

The sale of extraterrestrial real estate is nothing new; indeed, it's been around since the 1890s, well after Jules Verne wrote *From the Earth to the Moon*. One night in 1936, A. Dean Lindsay looked up at the Moon and declared, "My God, no one owns it." On June 15 of that year, Mr. Lindsay walked into a notary public office in Pittsburgh and made a claim of ownership over "all" extraterrestrial objects.

It is easy to write off these schemes as those of quacks, but we are entering an era when people are seriously advocating that the United States establish property rights on the Moon and scholars debate the legality of mining asteroids.

Real estate development in outer space may seem outlandish and futuristic, but it is certainly conceivable, even if at present it seems unrealistic. Considering the long history of real estate development, stretching from placemakers like Alexander the Great to Napoleon III and William Zeckendorf, and appreciating the obstacles real estate developers have had to hurdle over the ages, anything seems possible. Earlier generations had similar reactions when a set of developers turned the dry sand dunes of Nevada into Las Vegas, and unused cotton fields near Dallas into a massive shopping center. Engineer and futurist Buckminster Fuller imagined a visionary space car to travel easily back and forth between the Earth and space; with such a vehicle, shopping or living on the Moon, Mars and other planets, does not seem so distant. Perhaps Buckminster Fuller's car will do for the real estate development of outer space what Henry Ford's Model T did for the development of suburbia here on Earth.

## Afterword

"IS THERE A real estate developer gene?" A friend asked this question after reading a draft of this book, and similar questions have been asked by my students, seeking insight into the industry. In chapter 1 we tried to outline the reasons humans build and listed those characteristics that make for a good real estate developer, but as far as I know, there have been no studies to determine whether there really is a real estate developer gene, or whether the real estate development skill is inherited.

Real estate development is yet to be considered a true profession and few schools, if any, teach students how to become developers. Those universities that give courses in real estate development still fail to teach how one acquires creative talents such as vision, tenacity and the kind of chutzpah required to successfully conceptualize, orchestrate and realize major projects.

I have met dozens, if not hundreds, of real estate developers, and none of them has a degree in the subject. All of them, to my knowledge, came to the process through the school of hard knocks, combining ambition with determination. They have also come to the business from various backgrounds. I know real estate developers who started their careers as doctors, lawyers, architects, contractors, brokers, schoolteachers, military personnel, bureaucrats, clergy and, yes, even actors. Real estate development clearly requires both persistence and optimism in order to successfully face the many obstacles placed in front of the developer during the building process. But above all, it requires a vivid imagination to see what could be, and a commitment to make it happen.

Being a developer is a complex business that demands the ability to manage an array of human and financial resources and the talent to interact effectively with other people. The development process, though modified for each project, remains essentially the same as it has been since the development of the city of Uruk six thousand years ago. Success in real estate development is measured two ways: first, the quality of the project, especially its design, so that it will not quickly become obsolete, and second, the project's economic success. Rarely do the two measurements of success coincide. In addition, history reveals that achieving a great project requires a special relationship between the developer and his or her architect, as we have seen in the cases of Napoleon III and Baron Haussmann, Job Harriman and Alice Constance Austin, and William Zeckendorf and I.M. Pei.

In each case, the developer must possess impresario qualities that can emanate only from an individual, not a committee. Because of their preoccupation with their vision, developers who produce great buildings are usually more interested in the realization of their projects and not the economics. They are often accused of "marrying their projects," and in many cases, fail to abandon them in the face of overwhelming negative evidence. All too often they become bankrupt, their development business overtaken by bankers, lawyers or accountants who do not possess the developer's creative skills. The resulting projects, lacking the charismatic developer spirit, often become pedestrian in nature.

Many developers, whether doing large or small projects, try to do them with as little equity as possible and operate under the credo OPM (other people's money). When it comes to funding real estate projects, the highest-risk money and the most difficult money to secure is what is called "seed money." These are the funds needed to initiate a project, conceptualize it, option land, test the market and pay for myriad other things before the developer can secure construction financing and move the project toward completion.

Some developers, not related to large financial institutions or possessing their own reserve of funds, decide to "go public"—that is, become a public corporation and sell shares as a means of generating cash to be used, among other things, for seed money. Many of those who do go public end up reverting to private-company status because the rigors and constraints demanded of a public company are inconsistent with the typical developer's flamboyant style and the need to be able to make decisions quickly and be free to wheel and deal.

It is often said in real estate development circles that the second party coming into a deal makes the money, and this has often been the case. The creative developer conceives of a project, gets it going, loses it or is saved or bought out by a second party. The developer loses his or her equity, and the new purchaser, either because of greater financial resources or changes in the marketplace, is able to make a success of it.

In recent years, those who financed buildings decided they wanted to become developers. Consequently, insurance companies and pension funds and other institutions entered the field. But because they are institutions and conservative in nature, often they lack the imaginative panache needed to produce great buildings. In many cases, real estate developers have found themselves simply acting as consultants or development managers for large institutions. However, working for a large institution in a corporate climate is hardly the same as being your own boss.

Real estate development has always been, and will always remain, a high-risk, creative process. But we owe our built environment, the good and the bad, to those gutsy, imaginative entrepreneurs and placemakers who, throughout history, took the risks to make real estate development an essential, physical component of the social, cultural and economic texture of our cities.

## Acknowledgments

THIS BOOK STEMS FROM my sixty-plus years of experience in architecture and development but could not have happened if Judy Oberlander, founder of the City Program at British Columbia's Simon Fraser University, had not encouraged me to teach the course Real Estate Development from the Inside Out. The first night of the course includes a 100-mile-per-hour ride through real estate development history. Teaching the course and gathering information about the history of real estate development for seventeen years, and the encouragement of my regrettably departed friend Michael Fellman, professor of history at SFU, made the writing of this book possible.

The book, however, might not have been published without Simon Fraser University agreeing to raise the money required. In gratitude for this generous gesture, I and coauthor Ira Nadel have waived all royalties in favor of Simon Fraser University. We are indebted to Gordon Price and Frank Pacella of the university's City Program and the following who made donations toward the publishing of *Placemakers*.

SPONSORS: Michael Alexander and Dianna Waggoner, Michael Audain, Lisa and Ernest Auerbach Family Foundation, Bing Thom Architects Inc., Keith and Leslie Burrell, Intergulf Development Group, Edward (Ted) Johnson, Eric Martin, Power Corporation of Canada, John and Phyllis Rae, SFU Community Trust, the SFU 50th Anniversary Fund, and Dan Zhang and Three Bridges Properties Corp.

DONORS: Michael JB Alexander, Alan Bleviss, Gary and Joyce Follman, Norman and Gloria May, Judy and Philip O'Brien, Judith and Thomas Sebal, Barbara Rae and George Stuart, and Bryan and Audrey Williams.

*Placemakers* would not have come to fruition under the hands of this novice writer without the guidance, expertise, encouragement, patience and prodding of coauthor Ira Nadel. His contributions helped to give the book focus and clarity, and in responding to the detailed and professional demands of our publisher, Figure 1 Publishing, he helped to make this read and ride, although not at 100 miles per hour, a smooth one. Our work was enhanced by the meticulous editing of Naomi Pauls, Judy Phillips and Eva van Emden.

Helping Ira and me was the wonderful graphic artist Dragan Nikodijevic of Barcelona Media Design, who helped me convey to the publishers the aesthetic for *Placemakers* that I was looking for. John Calimente, a former student of my course, researched details and sought out the illustrations that grace these pages. And John Myers, intellectual property lawyer, provided sage advice and counsel. A special thank-you to all those individuals, museums and foundations that provided the rights of reproduction for the illustrations (for full credits, see page 197).

I must also thank the readers who reviewed early manuscripts and gave their candid and unmerciful critiques. They included real estate professionals Bob Penner, Michael Mortensen, John Ruskin and David Goldman; writers Lois Dubin, Lisa Bernie, Jay Hoffman and David Lemon; friends Anne Rowles, Kay James, Pam Turpin and Dr. Stan Lubin; and family members cousin Pam Gilfond, my children Marc, Michele, Paul and Andrew, and daughter-in-law Erica and especially Marc's partner, Alice Chesworth, whose dissecting and paring down of the original draft deserves special mention.

Last but not least, I offer a profound and loving thank-you to my late wife, Mary Allison James Auerbach, whose patience, assistance and encouragement during our past sixty years together have been without peer. She has deserved every ounce of my respect, and she has never failed to remind me that "behind every successful man is a surprised woman."

*Herb Auerbach*
VANCOUVER, B.C.

## Selected Bibliography

Achilles Tatius. *Leucippe and Clitophon*. Translated by S. Gaselee. Loeb Classical Library 45. Cambridge, MA: Harvard University Press, 1969.

Adler, Jerry. *High Rise: How 1,000 Men and Women Worked around the Clock for Five Years and Lost $200 Million Building a Skyscraper*. New York: HarperCollins, 1993.

Appleyard, Bryan. "Bedford Park: The Enchanted Suburb," *Sunday Times*, April 8, 2013. http://bryanappleyard.com/bedford-park-the-enchanted-suburb.

Arndt, Ingo. *Animal Architecture*. New York: Abrams, 2014.

Babbitt, Bruce. *Cities in the Wilderness: A New Vision of Land Use in America*. Washington, DC: Island Press, 2007.

Bedford Park Society. *A Short History of Bedford Park*. Bedford, UK: Bedford Park Society, 2003.

Bianco, Anthony. *The Reichmanns: Family, Faith, Fortune, and the Empire of Olympia & York*. Toronto: Random House, 1997.

Blumenfeld, Hans. *The Modern Metropolis: Its Origins, Growth, Characteristics, and Planning*. Cambridge, MA: MIT Press, 1971.

Braudel, Fernand. *Civilization and Capitalism, 15th–18th Century*. Vol. 1, *The Structures of Everyday Life*. Translated by Siân Reynolds. New York: Harper & Row, 1981.

Brown, Justine. *All Possible Worlds: Utopian Experiments in British Columbia*. Vancouver, BC: New Star Books, 1995.

Bryant, R.W.G. *Land: Private Property, Public Control*. Eugene, OR: Harvest House, 1972.

Campanella, Tommaso. *The City of the Sun*. Project Gutenberg. http://www.gutenberg.org/files/2816/2816-h/2816-h.htm.

Choi, Y.J. *East and West: Understanding the Rise of China*. Bloomington, IN: iUniverse, 2010.

Clark, Susan. "Powell River Townsite: A Craftsman-Era Company Town in the Canadian Wilderness." *American Bungalow* 60 (Winter 2008): 28–39.

Clegg, John A. *The History of Flagler County*. Flagler Beach, FL: Flagler County Historical Society, 1976.

Cueille, Sophie. *Le Vésinet: modèle français d'urbanisme paysager, 1858–1930*, Cahiers de l'inventaire, 17. Paris: Imprimerie nationale éditions, 1989.

Darley, Gillian. *Villages of Vision: A Study of Strange Utopias*. London: Architectural Press, 1975.

Davis, William Stearns. *A Day in Old Rome: A Picture of Roman Life*. New York: Biblio & Tannen, 1967.

De Soto, Hernando. *The Mystery of Capital: Why Capitalism Triumphs in the West and Fails Everywhere Else*. New York: Basic Books, 2000.

D'Souza, Aruna, and Tom McDonough, eds. *The Invisible Flâneuse? Gender, Public Space and Visual Culture in Nineteenth-Century Paris*. Manchester: Manchester University Press, 2008.

Eco, Umberto. *The Book of Legendary Lands*. New York: Rizzoli Ex Libris, 2013.

Editors, Charles River. *Grand Central Station: The History of New York City's Famous Railroad Terminal*. Kindle edition. 2015. http://www.amazon.ca/ Grand-Central-Station-Railroad-Terminal-ebook/dp/B00TG2UKGM.

Edwards, Trystan. *Good and Bad Manners in Architecture: An Essay on the Social Aspects of Civic Design*. London: Philip Allan, 1924.

*The Epic of Gilgamesh*. Translated by Maureen Gallery Kovacs. Academy for Ancient Texts. http://www.ancienttexts.org/library/mesopotamian/gilgamesh/ tab1.htm.

Fellman, Michael. *The Unbounded Frame: Freedom and Community in Nineteenth Century American Utopianism*. Westport, CT: Greenwood Press, 1973.

Ford, David Nash. "Tudor London." *Britannia*. 2013. http://www.britannia.com/ history/londonhistory/tudlon.html.

Gans, Herbert, J. *The Levittowners: Ways of Life and Politics in a New Suburban Community*. New York: Pantheon Books, 1967.

Gillette, King Camp. *The Human Drift*. Austin, TX: New Era Publishing, 1894.

Haberman, Ian S. *The Van Sweringens of Cleveland: The Biography of an Empire*. Cleveland: Western Reserve Historical Society, 1979.

Hammer, Richard. *The Helmsleys: The Rise and Fall of Harry and Leona Helmsley*. New York: Plume, 1990.

Hansell, Mike. *Built by Animals: The Natural History of Animal Architecture*. Oxford: Oxford University Press, 2007.

Hayden, Dolores. *Seven American Utopias: The Architecture of Communitarian Socialism, 1790–1975*. Cambridge, MA: MIT Press, 1979.

———. *The Grand Domestic Revolution: A History of Feminist Designs for American Homes, Neighborhoods, and Cities*. Cambridge, MA: MIT Press, 1981.

Hayward, Maria. "Rich Pickings: Henry VIII's Use of Confiscation and Its Significance for the Development of the Royal Collection." In *Henry VIII and the Court: Art, Politics and Performance*, edited by Thomas Betteridge and Suzannah Lipscomb, 29–46. Farnham, UK: Ashgate, 2013.

Helman, Claire. *The Milton-Park Affair: Canada's Largest Citizen-Developer Confrontation*. Montreal: Véhicule Press, 1987.

Horne, Alistair. *La Belle France*. New York: Knopf, 2005.

"An Interactive Exhibit Chronicles the History of Building Blocks." Fastcodesign.com, http://www.fastcodesign.com/1671326/an-interactive-exhibit-chronicles- the-history-of-building-blocks.

Jacobs, Jane. *Cities and the Wealth of Nations*. New York: Vintage, 1985.

Kotkin, Joel. *The City: A Global History*. New York: Modern Library, 2005.

Krakauer, Jon. *Under the Banner of Heaven: A Story of Violent Faith*. New York: Anchor Books, 2003.

Laffont, Robert et Jacques Boudet. *Histoire de Paris et des Parisiens*. Paris: Editions du Pont Royal, 1958.

La Rocca, Eugenio, Cécile Giroire, Daniel Roger, Annalisa Lo Monaco and Claudio Parisi Presicce. *Auguste*. Exhibition catalogue for *Moi, Auguste, Empereur de Rome* at the Galeries nationales, Grand Palais. Paris: Réunion des musées nationaux, 2014.

"The L'Enfant and McMillan Plans." National Park Service, U.S. Department of the Interior, n.d. http://www.nps.gov/nr/travel/wash/lenfant.htm.

Lorimer, James. *The Developers*. Toronto: James Lorimer & Company, 1978.

McPhee, John. *Annals of the Former World*. New York: Farrar, Straus and Giroux, 1998.

Mohney, David, and Keller Easterling, eds. *Seaside: Making a Town in America*. New York: Princeton Architectural Press, 1991.

Morris, William. *Collected Letters of William Morris*. Vol. 1, *1848–1880*, edited by Norman Kelvin. Princeton, NJ: Princeton University Press, 1984.

———. *Hopes and Fears for Art*. London: Ellis & White, 1882. https://ebooks.adelaide.edu.au/m/morris/william/m87hf/complete.html.

Mumford, Lewis. *The City in History: Its Origins, Its Transformations, and Its Prospects*. Boston: Mariner Books, 1968.

Murray, Peter. "Bedford Park and the Aesthetic Movement." Bedford Park Society, March 28, 2011. http://neighbournet.com/server/common/bedfordparksociety001.htm.

Natelson, Robert G. "Comments on the Historiography of Condominium: The Myth of Roman Origin." *Oklahoma City University Law Review* 12, no. 1 (Spring 1987): 17–58. http://scholarship.law.umt.edu/cgi/viewcontent.cgi?article=1042&context=faculty_lawreviews.

Nisbet, Robert. *The Social Philosophers: Community and Conflict in Western Thought*. New York: Thomas Y. Crowell, 1973.

Orlin, Lena Cowen. *Locating Privacy in Tudor England*. Oxford: Oxford University Press, 2007.

Pacelle, Mitchell. *Empire: A Tale of Obsession, Betrayal, and the Battle for an American Icon*. New York: Wiley, 2002.

Pagnano, Giuseppe. *Grammichele — Luoghi di Sicilia* [Grammichele — Places of Sicily]. Translated by Denis Gailor. Edizioni Ariete. Palermo: Kalós Press, [1998].

"Paris Modernization." *Travel to Europe's Heart* (December 7, 2012), http://traveltoeuropesheart.com/paris-modernization.

Peel, Lucy, Polly Powell and Alexander Garrett. *An Introduction to 20th-Century Architecture*. Secaucus, NJ: Chartwell Books, 1989.

Pipes, Richard. *Property and Freedom*. New York: Vintage Books, 2000.

Plato. *The Republic*. Project Gutenberg. http://www.gutenberg.org/files/1497/1497-h/1497-h.htm.

Plutarch. [*Life of*] *Alexander*. Translated by John Dryden. Internet Classics Archive. http://classics.mit.edu/Plutarch/alexandr.html.

———. [*Life of*] *Crassus*. Translated by John Dryden. Internet Classics Archive. http://classics.mit.edu/Plutarch/crassus.html.

Polanyi, Karl. *The Great Transformation: The Political and Economic Origins of Our Time*. Boston: Beacon Press, 1944.

Rachlis, Eugene, and John E. Marqusee. *The Landlords*. New York: Random House, 1963.

Rudofsky, Bernard. *Architecture without Architects: A Short Introduction to Non-Pedigreed Architecture*. New York: Doubleday, 1964.

Rykwert, Joseph. *The Idea of a Town: The Anthropology of Urban Form in Rome, Italy and the Ancient World*. Cambridge, MA: MIT Press, 1988.

Sakolski, Aaron M. *The Great American Land Bubble: The Amazing Story of Land-Grabbing, Speculations, and Booms from Colonial Days to the Present Time*. Mansfield Center, CT: Martino Fine Books, 2011.

Sen, Amartya. *Development as Freedom*. Reprint ed. New York: Anchor Books, 2000.

Shaw, Norman. ["Bedford Park"]. *The Victorian Web*. N.d. http://www.victorianweb.org/art/architecture/normanshaw/7.html.

Smith, George D. *Nauvoo Polygamy: "…But We Called It Celestial Marriage."* Salt Lake City: Signature Books, 2011.

Thompson, E.P. The *Making of the English Working Class*. London: Victor Gollancz, 1963.

Toynbee, Arnold. *Cities of Destiny*. New York: McGraw-Hill, 1967.

Trump, Donald J. with Tony Schwartz. *Trump: The Art of the Deal*. Reprint ed. New York: Ballantine Books, 2004.

United Nations Office for Outer Space Affairs. *United Nations Treaties and Principles on Outer Space, Related General Assembly Resolutions and Other Documents*. N.d. http://www.unoosa.org/pdf/misc/SpaceLaw/STSPACE-61Rev1_-_English.pdf.

Wallace, William. *The Transformation of Western Europe*. London: Royal Institute of International Affairs, 1990.

Ward, Barbara. *Human Settlements: Crisis and Opportunity*. Ottawa: Information Canada, 1974.

Wegner, Phillip. *Imaginary Communities: Utopia, the Nation and the Spatial Histories of Modernity*. Berkeley: University of California Press, 2002.

Wilson, R. "Idealism and the Origin of the First American Suburb: Llewellyn Park, New Jersey." *American Art* 11, no. 4 (Fall 1979): 79–93.

Zeckendorf, William, with Edward McCreary. *The Autobiography of William Zeckendorf*. New York: Holt, Rinehart & Winston, 1970.

# Index

Photographs indicated by
page numbers in italics

Brooklyn-born HERB AUERBACH started his career as a stage designer. He attended Pratt Institute, where he secured both a degree in architecture and a commission as an officer in the U.S. Army Corps of Engineers. Herb was stationed in France and remained there for four years. He then returned to New York City and the office of I.M. Pei & Associates, soon becoming resident architect for Place Ville Marie in Montreal, a signature development of William Zeckendorf. He later became VP of development for Concordia Estates and president of its subsidiary Descon/Concordia, a firm pioneering new building systems. In Montreal, he cofounded the Centaur Theatre and is a life governor of the National Theatre School of Canada. In Vancouver, he founded the Bill Reid Foundation and its Bill Reid Gallery of Northwest Coast Art. Herb currently teaches a course on real estate development at Simon Fraser University, Vancouver.

IRA NADEL is the author of biographies of Leonard Cohen, Tom Stoppard, David Mamet and Leon Uris. With the San Francisco architect Donald MacDonald, he has published books on the Golden Gate Bridge, Alcatraz and the new Bay Bridge between Oakland and San Francisco. His other publications focus on James Joyce, Ezra Pound, Gertrude Stein and, most recently, 9/11. He is professor of English at the University of British Columbia, Vancouver.